The front cover illustration is a previously unpublished painting by Napoleon Primo Vallejo, General Vallejo's son and 16th child. The artist born in 1850, painted this image of Mission Dolores in the 1880s, when he lived on Dolores street.

Image courtesy of the Barbara Koerper Collection

MISSION DOLORES

The Gift of St. Francis

First in a Series on the Missions of California

Misión de Nuestro Sera Pico Padre San Francisco de Asís
a la Laguna de los Dolores

By
Brother Guire Cleary, S.S.F.
Curator, Mission San Francisco de Asís

The Paragon Agency
Publishers
2004

MISSION DOLORES

The Gift of St. Francis

Cleary, Br. Guire, S.S.F. 1951—

Published by
The Paragon Agency
Orange, California
2004

1. Mission Dolores
2. California Missions
3. California History
   I. Title
   II. Author

ISBN: 1-891030-40-X

Printed in the USA
1k, r3

DEDICATION

Dedicated to Scott Yee who taught me to listen for all the voices in a story and not just the loudest speaker.

A portion of the proceeds of this book are given to Mission Dolores, through the generocity of the author.

ACKNOWLEDGMENTS

This book and my remarkable experiences at Mission Dolores would not have been possible without the support of the people and staff of Mission Dolores. The author would specifically like to thank Fathers John J. O'Connor, Maurice "Mickey" McCormick and William J. Justice who stand in the sandals of Fray Francisco Palóu. The work of scholars such as, Marie Duggan, Malcolm Margolian and Randall Milliken, colleagues and friends at the Archeology Lab at the Presidio of San Francisco, the San Francisco History Association, the California Mission Studies Association and the San Francisco Historical Society have been vital to opening the eyes and the ears of my imagination and recapturing the voices of nearly forgotten peoples; Indian, Spanish and even Irish Americans. The dedication of Indian descendants, amateur scholars, docents and volunteers has informed, supported and inspired me on a daily basis. My heartfelt thanks to such wonderful people as Andy Galvan, Bob Huerta, Pat Lynch, Aaron Olivas and Joan Sexton. Their stories are just as extraordinary as those in this book.

Brother Guire Cleary, S.S.F.

CONTENTS

PREFACE

A wooden stick with two prongs found in a cabinet, a yellowed piece of lace found in a box and a people without recognition: these were the almost forgotten voices that captured me as Curator of San Francisco's historic Mission Dolores. The stick turned out to be an Indian musical instrument and the lace was determined to be a piece of handiwork by a woman of Mission Dolores made after the Great Earthquake and Fire of 1906. The Ohlone Indians are still a people unrecognized by the United States government.

The missions of California have been a delight for visitors for two centuries. But so often the study and understanding of these wonderful places forgets that they were places made by people and who had thousands of stories and whose memory is almost forgotten. Their voices are often tattered bits of wood or fabric or fading photographs. The Spanish writer Valle Inclán wrote, "Things are not as we see them but how we remember them." How fragile is memory and how easily the voices of ordinary people living extraordinary lives are lost. It is the work of the historian to produce a kind of magic: bringing back the voices of children, women and men to speak to us of what they experienced.

Over the computer screen in my mission office is a quote from Malcolm Margolian. At least once a day I read, "...today's carefully restored missions do not portray history. Rather in the manner of 'theme parks' they use the ornaments of history to create a soothing world of fantasy." It is my hope that within this book you will hear the voices of 225 years of people building, praying, working, suffering, playing and living within the adobe walls of this place, Mission San Francisco de Asís in the Village of Chutchui. They speak to us today if we but listen.

Br. Guire Cleary, S. S. F.
January, 2004

[Feast of the Manifestation of Christ to the Magi and the Gentiles]

FOREWORD

During the summer of 2003, I was in San Francisco. Contacting the San Francisco Museum & Historical Society and the Historic Association, I was informed that Brother Guire would be giving his last tour of the Mission Cemetery and Gardens — that evening. He was transferring after the first of the year, and this would be the last opportunity to take the tour with him.

With the tour only a few hours away, I took the local trolly (the railway with the electrical wire overhead that trollies behind,) up to Dolores Street and walked down the three blocks to the Mission.

I've been on many tours, given by many so-called experts. Usually I find their grasp of history is limited, a product of the tours being given by docents and volunteers. Our tour guide was however, Br. Guire.

He spoke with vision, and painted a wide canvas of the interplay between the Native Americans, the Padres and the Soldiers. This was early San Francisco — the beginnings of a great city, and his story was a story of passion.

Br. Guire continued the tour, for much longer than I believe was normally done. Perhaps being the last tour, made it more important. After the tour was finally over, people stood around and asked questions. Only after all had gone did I approach Br. Guire, introducing myself as a historical publisher.

We talked while he closed up the Mission, and I followed him around, watching him lock doors and return display items to their cases. We left by the back way and walked toward his home. We talked of the people that once lived here and how a Mission grew into a vibrant city.

By the time we reached his doorstep, we had agreed on publishing this book. Br. Guire ran inside and brought me a manuscript, one that he had been working on for some time. He said he would follow up with illustrations and we could communicate by the internet.

Over the next six months we corresponded about content, changes, updates, new illustrations and many other elements. All to produce what is here in this book.

Br. Guire wrote with vision, and again he painted a wide canvas of early San Francisco. His story is a story of passion and Brother Guire has written this great book.

Many of the illustrations in this book, have never been published before and few have ever been within the same volume. The cover illustration also has never before been published — but came from a different source entirely.

A good friend of mine, Hank Koerper, lives in the town of Orange, as I do. He teaches anthropology at a local college and happened to be over showing me something he found on the history of baseball.

The cover we were using for this book, had a colored post card for an illustration. This is commonly done and I wasn't impressed with the outcome thus far, but I had little else from which to choose.

Hank told me his mother had a painting of the Mission Dolores, painted by none other than a son of General Mariano Vallejo — Napoleon. He brought me a small photo of the painting and I told him that if we could get the painting in time, I would use it on the cover, probably the back.

At Christmas, Hank drove up to his mother's home and brought back the painting. I sent it out to be scanned and Hank drove the painting back up a few days later.

While Hank was gone the second time, I received the scan back from the service bureau. It was incredible. The richness of the color was superb, the style was that of 1880s California, and the artist was someone who had a place in California history. Only later did I discover that he lived on Dolores Street when he painted this work.

Of course I removed the post card cover and replace it with the illustration of the painting, as it is now. Brother Guire was very happy with the new choice and informed me that Napoleon was his neighbor, if only a century apart.

As I publish, I continue to see the miracles that bring books together. That the cover artist was a neighbor of the author and that painting came through a neighbor of the publisher. And it all started because during the summer of 2003, I was in San Francisco.

Douglas Westfall, Publisher
January, 2004

BIOGRAPHY

Brother Guire Cleary, S.S.F., is a Franciscan friar of the Episcopal Church and holds an M.A. in history. After a number of years as a business litigation paralegal, he decided to return to his religious community. His life experience includes retail sales, owning a green grocery and serving as the Assistant Director of a refugee resettlement agency. In 1999 Br. Guire was appointed Curator of historic Mission San Francisco de Asís (Mission Dolores,) the first Franciscan brother to serve at that historic California Mission since 1845. That he happens to an Anglican serving on the staff of a Roman Catholic institution is a hopeful sign of both ecumenism and irony. During Br. Guire's tenure as Curator, Mission Dolores increased its programs in history to more than 10,000 students per year, worked to increase cooperation among educational, museum and historical associations, public advocacy of diversity in historical perspective, and honoring and working with the First Peoples of California. Br. Guire has also served on the boards of directors of the San Francisco History Association and the California Mission Studies Association. He is the recipient of several awards including Friend of the Ohlone People, Honorary U.S. Park Ranger and the Oscar Lewis Award for historical writing. Concluding his time at Mission Dolores in February 2004, he relinquished the position of Curator to a California Mission Indian descendant, thus becoming the first Franciscan friar at a California Mission to turn over management of one of the historic missions to an Indian and the first Franciscan friar at a California Mission to have an Indian as his boss. Br. Guire began as a volunteer.

"Go and do thou likewise."

Brother Guire Cleary, S.S.F.

INTRODUCTION
Of Missions and Harbors

Padre Presidente Junípero Serra

A story is told by the first Franciscan missionary at Mission Dolores and California's first historian, Fray Francisco Palóu, about the naming of San Francisco. In 1768, when José de Gálvez, Inspector General of Mexico, told the Franciscan President of the Missions, Fray Junípero Serra that he had decided to name the first three missions to be established in Alta California after San Diego, San Antonio and San Carlos the Franciscan protested saying, "Sir, and is there to be no mission for Our Father St. Francis?" de Gálvez laughed and said, "If St. Francis desires a mission in his honor, let him see to it that his harbor is located, and his name shall be given to it."

In 1769 an overland party set out from Mexico to explore Monterey Bay under the command of Captain Gaspár de Portolá. They arrived at the site, looked at their maps, scratched their heads and wondered, "Is this Monterey Bay?" With 17 of the 64 men sick and provisions quickly being consumed the expedition held a meeting on the feast day of Saint Francis, October 4, 1769, to decide whether to continue or return to Mexico. They decided to push forward. On October 22 they had the first recorded encounter between Europeans and Ohlone people. They encountered Quiroste Ohlone at the village of Mitenne near today's Point Año Nuevo. The Ohlone people cheered the explorers and showed traditional hospitality by offering food and tobacco. To Sergeant Francisco Ortega they made a present of a red colored staff decorated with

Original artist's design by the Franz Mayer Co., for a window of Junípero Serra at the Mission Dolores Basilica. This design was not utilized.
Collection of Mission Dolores

feathers. On November 1, 1769, Sergeant Ortega climbed up what is now called Sweeney Ridge, looked down and saw San Francisco Bay. Saint Francis had led the Spanish Empire to one of the largest harbors in the world. Now this place in the land of the Ohlone would have a mission for Saint Francis.

In March of 1772 Lieutenant Pedro Fages explored the harbor of San Francisco Bay and saw whales swimming within the bay and wrote that this grand harbor could hold "all the ships of Spain." Even though European explorers had been sailing up and down the coast of California for some 200 years they had never sighted the passage through the mountains we call the Golden Gate and the huge bays behind it because of the fog and the position of Angel Island.

The story of how San Francisco got its name begins with a challenge and a joke. San Francisco is a place of story telling and tales can be as tall as the Redwoods. It is said that Gálvez had many strange ideas and once considered the possibility of using monkeys as soldiers in his army. No wonder the City of Saint Francis is often tolerant of crazy ideas! No idea is too crazy for a San Franciscan to think about or at least long enough to laugh.

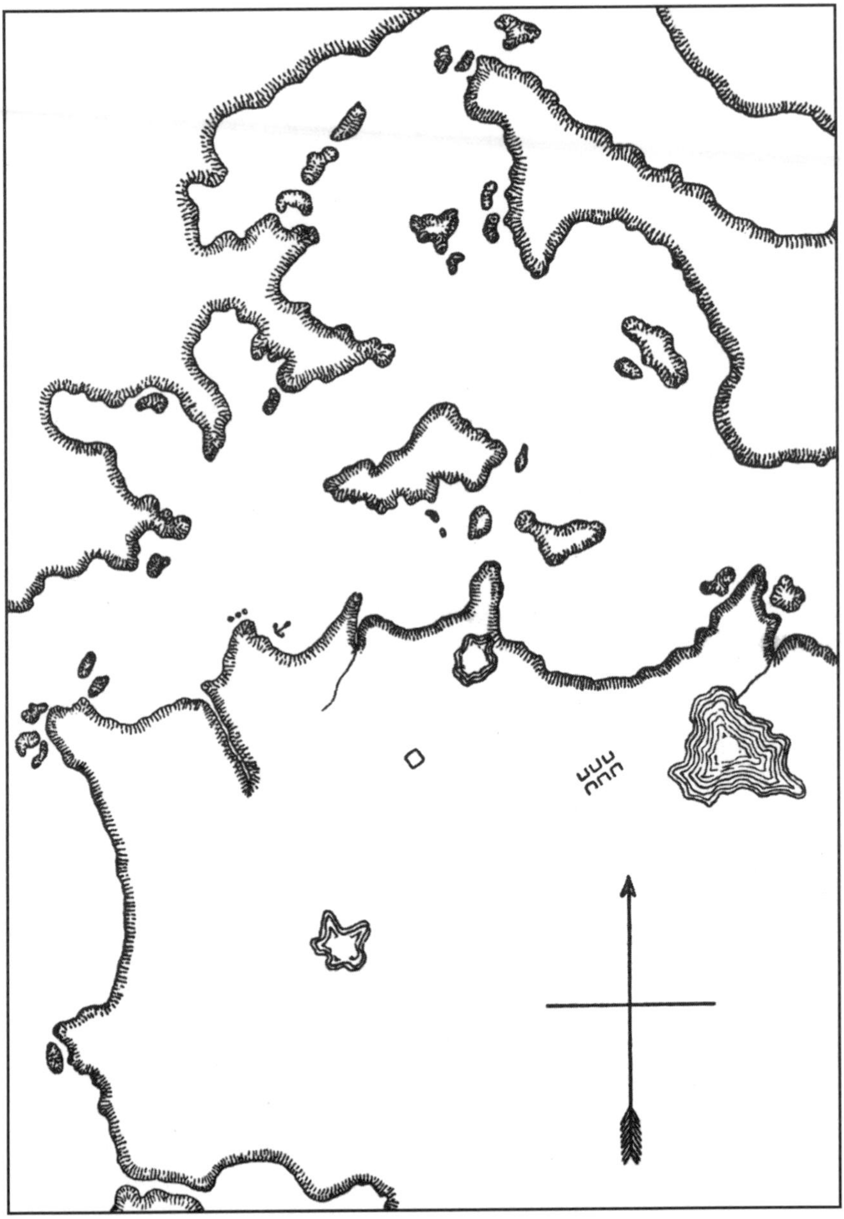

"The French Admiral, La Pérouse, touched at Monterey, in September 1786, he dispatched some of his officers to the Port of San Francisco, who made a chart of that Bay, which was sent to France, and was published with the account of his explorations upt to that point, and is thus preserved to us."

San Francisco In its 100th Year – The Paragaon Agency, 2004

CHAPTER 1
The Gift of St. Francis

The Mission and Presidio of Our Father San Francisco

On a summer day like to every other summer day for thousands of years something new entered the small Ohlone village of Chutchui. A party of some 193 men, women and children from Mexico had arrived at the banks of a small lake they called "Angel Island." With them were soldiers on horseback, 1,000 head of cattle, guns, hammers, knives and other tools of iron and other remarkable things: as well as ideas as to government, ownership, morality, civilization and religion. The eternal cycles of dry season and wet season and the rhythms of individual lives paced off by birth, maturity, marriage, childbearing, and death were confronted by clocks and almanacs. The sameness of each day to another day was broken by the arrival of the calendar and the date on the calendar was June 27, 1776. The Spanish Empire, led by Lt. José Joaquín Moraga and Fray Francisco Palóu had arrived to establish the Mission and Presidio of Our Holy Father Saint Francis in the port of the same name in Alta California during the reign of his Catholic Majesty, Carlos III. The stone age hunter-harvester cultures of this region were challenged by the high technology culture of the Spanish Empire *encuentro* that spanned continents, utilized tools and instruments of steel, was aware of first experiments in electricity, participated in an expanding world economy and had centuries of organizational experience on a global scale and stood at the dawn of the Industrial

Revolution, the Enlightenment and the democratic revolutions of the United States and France. Soon the grass huts of some 60

Photograph showing 1790 redwood beams holding up the roof of Mission Dolores with original rawhide lashing.
Collection of Mission Dolores.

Ohlone Indians living at Chutchui were to give way to a new village, Mission San Francisco de Asís.

Under a shelter made from the branches of trees *(enramada)* built by Moraga's soldiers, Fray Francisco Palóu celebrated the first Mass on the feast of Saints Peter and Paul, June 29, 1776. The soldiers remained about a month and withdrew to found the Royal Presidio near the Golden Gate. One can only guess at the emotions of perhaps anxiety, curiosity and excitement as Palóu and his small party watched the bulk of the settlers march three miles away leaving them with Indians of whom they knew little and with whom they had but a few words of common vocabulary. It was soon discovered that the Baja California Indian brought as a translator did not understand the Ohlone language! The missionaries turned their attention to the establishment of the mission and the conversion of Ohlone Indians in the nearby village of Chutchui. Palóu inscribed the Baptismal Register of the mission on August 1, 1776 with the words:

"The Mission of Our Father San Francisco, founded by Religious of the Holy Apostolic College of San Fernando at this Port of the same name of our Father San Francisco in Northern California, through the favor and at the expense of our Catholic Monarch, the King of Spain, Don Carlos III commenced at the same time that it was founded in the vicinity of the new presidio of the same name of San Francisco."

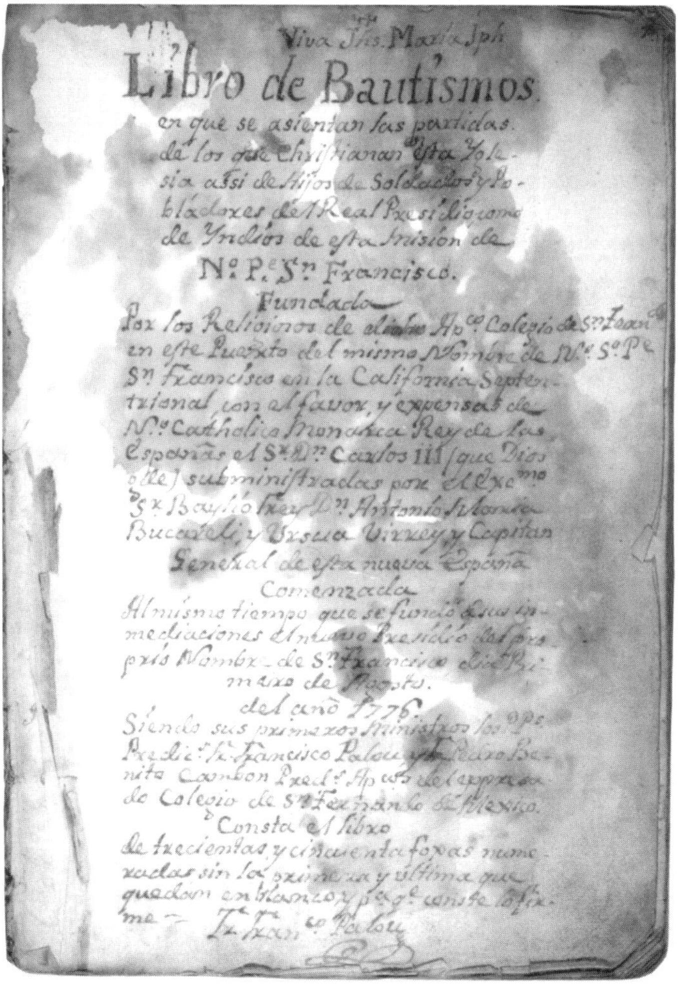
Viva Jhs. María Jph
Libro de Bautismos
en que se asientan las partidas
de los que christianan esta Yglesia
N.º P.e S.n Francisco.
Fundado
Comenzada
del año 1776.
Consta el libro

Title page from the first volume of Baptisms at Mission Dolores. It is in the handwriting of Fray Francisco Palóu and is dated August 1, 1776.
Collection of Mission Dolores

The mission was formally opened on October 9, 1776 with prayers, the setting up of a cross, firing of guns and the decoration of the church with signal flags from the ship. The foundation of the mission was coupled with the foundation of the Presidio. This relationship between religious and military was one of mutual dependence and also frequent antagonism as to differing goals and methods. Less than two weeks after Palóu wrote his inscription in his Book of Baptisms, Ohlone from what is now San Mateo attacked an Ohlone village near the newly established mission. The Indians near Lake Dolores were defeated and fled to what is now Marin and Contra Costa counties leaving the area even more depopulated. The total Indian population of what is now San Francisco may have been fewer than 300 people at the time of the Spanish *entrada*. Hostilities between Spanish soldiers and Ohlone in December 1776 caused the remaining Ohlone population to avoid Mission San Francisco until March 1777. It would seem the new mission was already a failure. Yet, somehow the first adult Indian baptism took place on June 24, 1777 when Chamis, a 20-year-old Ohlone man, was baptized and given the Christian name of Francisco Moraga with Lieut. Moraga acting as godfather. Chamis later became the first Indian married at Mission Dolores taking Paszém as his wife on April 24,1778. The Marriage Register recording their marriage is still in the collection of Mission Dolores. The priest who blessed this first marriage of Christian Indians at San Francisco was Francisco Palóu. Fray Palóu was deeply impressed with the tenderness of Indian families and wrote:

> *"...many married couples, both young and old, live together in the most perfect union and peacefulness, loving their children dearly, as the children their parents."*

Sometimes a small thing sets into motion many other things that eventually results in a very big thing. What could be more small than a cup of tea, but there is a story here. Russian people love to drink tea. The tea they loved came from China and the Chinese wanted the beautiful furs that the Russians had to trade. The furs came from Pacific sea otters and by 1745 Russians were hunting otters off the coast of California. This was making the King of Spain and his viceroy in Mexico very nervous. Although Spain had no settlements in Alta California, they did not want the Russians or anyone else to take away what they thought was part of their Empire. Also, the Spanish Empire needed a harbor to provision and protect its ships sailing from the Philippine Islands to Mexico.

Viceroy Antonio de Bucareli ordered Capitan Juan Bautista de Anza to recruit soldiers and settlers in Sonora, Mexico and establish a Mission and Royal Presidio in the port of San Francisco. Who were the men and women who came on the De Anza Expedition? Mostly they were women and children. Perhaps their life had been very difficult because there had been a drought in their homelands in Sonora for some ten years. Perhaps only someone very desperate would leave their home to walk more than a thousand miles to a world completely different than their own. But there was the hope of new land and a fresh

1790s bells hanging in the facade of Mission Dolores as seen from the attic. These bells are still lashed to their yokes with rawhide.

Collection of Mission Dolores

Center bell of Mission Dolores still held in place by rawhide thongs. This bell was made in Mexico in 1792.
Collection of Mission Dolores

start to give them courage. Where would Captain De Anza and his second-in-command Lieutenant Moraga lead them and what would they find?

Explorations

In 1774, an expedition led by Captain Fernando Rivera y Moncada began explorations for a suitable site for the mission and presidio of San Francisco. Accompanying the expedition was Fray Francisco Palóu. Presents were made to Ssalson Ohlone of beads and Spanish food, including wheat and beans.

Palóu records in his diary that the Indians were much taken with the products of European culture and Palóu promised that he would return and help the First Peoples to plant seeds and gather them in great abundance. Palóu believed that the Ohlone were pleased, understood him and would help build houses when he came back. This was the method of conversion in California: Indians would be attracted by European technology and culture and establishing their homes near missions, would ultimately accept Christianity and Spanish rule. On August 5, 1775 the Spanish naval vessel *San Carlos* became the first Spanish ship to enter San Francisco Bay, commanded by Captain Juan Bautista de Ayala and having Fray Vicente de Santa Maria as chaplain and missionary. The records of this exploration show a fascinating view of the natives of San Francisco Bay as courteous, awed by the wealth of Spanish culture and warmly human. At one point Fr. Santa Maria displayed a small statue of San Francisco de Asís, which the Huchuin men kissed with such devotion that Santa Maria wrote, "They stole my heart and

Original painting by Fr. John Giuliani, St. Francis of Assisi holding the Old Mission and Basilica welcomed by Chamis and Paszém. Commissioned in honor of the 225 anniversary of the establishment of San Francisco, 2001. Collection of Br. Guire Cleary, S.S.F.

Original artist's design by the Franz Mayer Co. For a window of Francisco Palóu at the Mission Dolores Basilica.

Collection of Mission Dolores

the hearts of all who observed them." An amazing meeting took place on Angel Island on the afternoon of August 24, 1775. The eight Huchuin men, possibly tribal ambassadors, took out rattles and began singing what Santa Maria believed to be sacred songs with tears in their eyes. At the conclusion, they handed the Franciscan priest their clapping sticks and indicated he should sing as well. In response Santa Maria sang the beloved Spanish hymn, "*Alabado*." Nineteen years later four of these men would be baptized at Mission Dolores. How different would our California have been if relations between peoples had continued to be in that spirit of sharing and song.

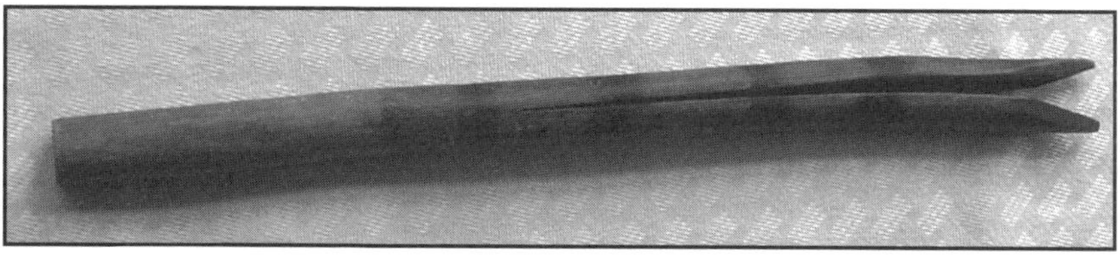

Ohlone clapping stick. One similar to this was probably used during the meeting between the Indian ambassadors and Fray Vicente de Santa Maria in 1774.
Collection of Mission Dolores

One early Franciscan explorer, Fray Pedro Font, recorded his love of nature, his enchantment with the land of Alta California and his hopes for the marvelous port of St. Francis. Looking out over the Bay from what is now the Presidio he wrote that no place in his travels had ever pleased him more and that

A small 18th century statue of San Francisco de Asís. Statues such as this were popular devotional items and it is probably a statue similar to this that was displayed to the Huchuin Indians in San Francisco Bay by Fray Vicente de Santa Maria in August 1775.
Collection of the Society of St. Francis

Coronation of the Blessed Mother by the Holy Trinity.
An 18th century oil painting brought from Mexico.
Collection of Mission Dolores

this port could be more beautiful than any in the world if settled like Europe. He described the discovery and naming of Dolores, "Passing through wooded hills and over flats with good lands in which we encountered two lagoons and some springs of good water, with plentiful grass, fennel and other useful herbs, we arrived at the beautiful arroyo which because it was Friday of Sorrows, we called the Arroyo de los Dolores. On its banks we found much and very fragrant manzanita and other plants and many wild violets. I concluded that the place was very pretty and the best for the establishment of one of the two missions." Mission San Francisco de Asís has as its nickname "Mission Dolores" which is taken from the name of the now vanished Lake Dolores and Dolores Creek.

SAN FRANCISCO

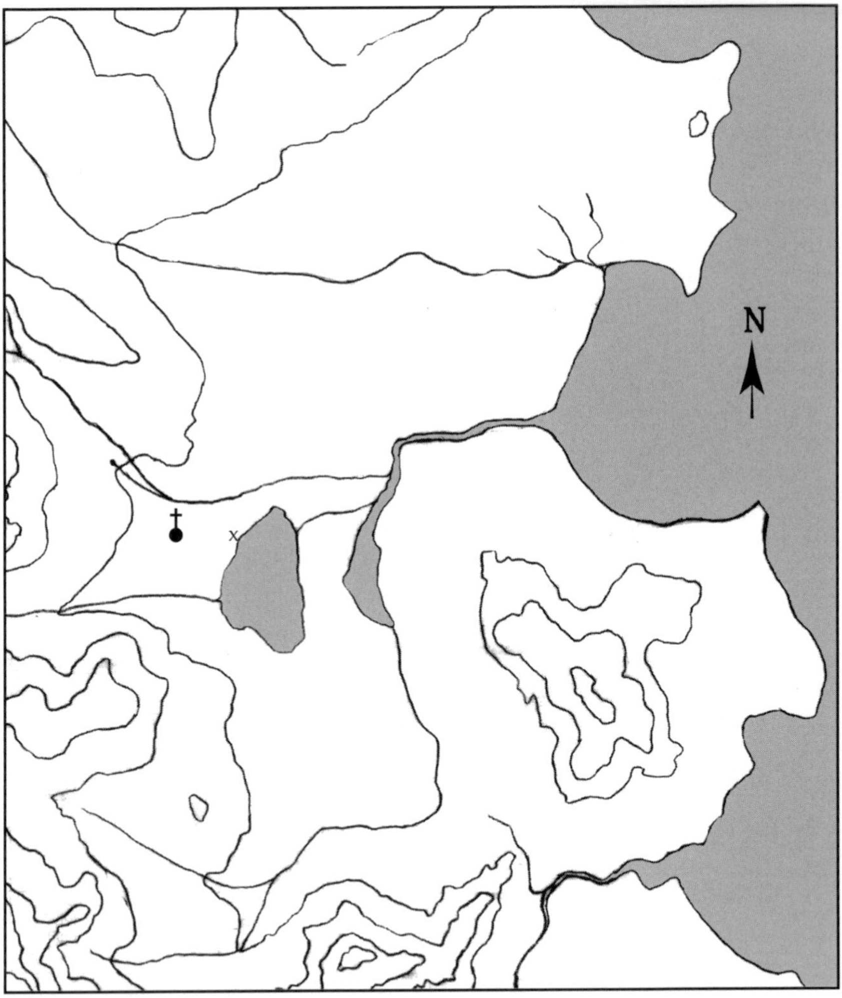

Map of San Francisco headland at the time of the founding of Mission Dolores. The "x" shows the first location near the lake.

CHAPTER 2
Three Voices

The Ohlone, the Franciscans, and the Soldiers

Mission Dolores is where San Francisco began in 1776. This little church made of mud-brick is the birthplace of our city. But there are many stories about our beginnings and our people. Some stories are of the soldiers and settlers who came from what is now Arizona and Mexico to find new homes and to extend the Spanish Empire. Some stories are of the Franciscan padres who wanted to build a community where God would be discovered among the Indian Peoples. Oldest and first are the stories of the Ohlone Indians because they and the other Indian nations of California are the First Peoples. The history of the Spanish settlement in California is less than 250 years old. The history of the California Indians is over 12,000 years old. These are three voices and three stories about our beginnings.

A souvenir guide to Mission Dolores. This was said to have been designed by Mrs. A.S. Forbes who promoted the placement of bells along El Camino Real.
c. 1920.
Collection of Mission Dolores

The Ohlone

Coyote was the first and wisest of the animals. His children became the race of human beings. Coyote was a good father and gave his children many gifts. He gave them tools to hunt birds, and animals and fish. His greatest gift was intelligence to see food everywhere in acorns, seeds and roots. The Elders discovered the healing goodness in plants. Everywhere: in the air, in the land and in the water there was food for Coyote's children. They would gather these things and never be hungry. [Ohlone creation story.]

Lithograph based on an 1816 sketch by Louis Choris showing Ohlone Indians dancing in front of Mission Dolores on the Feast of St. Francis. This is the oldest known image of Mission Dolores.

Bancroft Library, University of California at Berkeley

The world of the Ramaytush Ohlone was one of living with the seasons of nature: hunting, fishing, gathering. Baskets were woven from plant material and tools were made from stone and bone. Within a few hundred feet of today's Mission Dolores was a small village of perhaps 60 Ohlone people alongside a small creek in a village called Chutchui. Sometimes these people were called "Yelamu" and the Spanish called them, "Costanoan." In all of what we now call San Francisco there were perhaps only 250 Ohlone. They had lived on this peninsula since about the year 500 C.E.

Lithograph based on an 1816 sketch by Louis Choris showing Indians playing games in front of their homes. These adobe houses were sited directly across from Mission Dolores.
Library of Congress

Before the Ohlone people were the Hokan people who had lived on this bit of land for perhaps 5,000 years. Before that were only the animals on the land, the birds in the sky and the fish in the bay and creeks. Of the Ohlone people who were living at the time of the Spanish entry into the area (in Spanish "*entrada*") we know the names of a few and can guess at their lives. We know of a young man named Chamis who hunted rabbits, fished and made tools from bone or obsidian. There was the young girl who became his wife named Paszém. We can imagine her crushing acorns in a stone bowl to make acorn soup. Another woman was Huítpote. Perhaps like many Indian

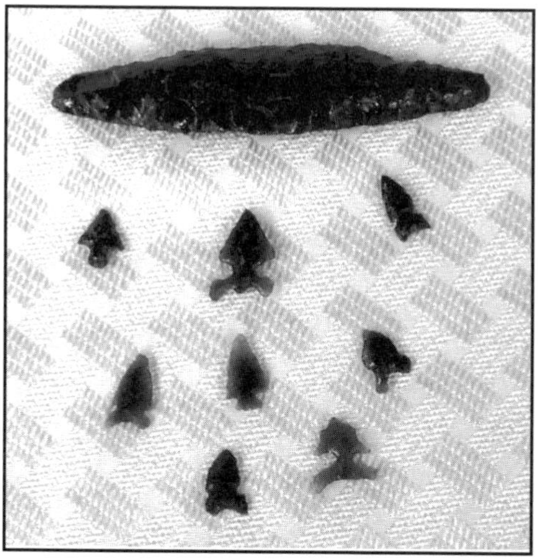

Miwok spearhead and arrow heads made from obsidian. Tools of the California Indians were often made from this material.
Collection of Mission Dolores

A California Indian willow leaf basket with acorns. Willow leaf baskets were preferred for food storage because they are insect resistant.
Collection of Mission Dolores

women she could weave a basket so tightly that it could hold water. Chamis, Pazém and Huítpote were real Ohlone who lived in the village of Chutchui when their world changed forever and a new world was born when the Spanish Empire arrived.

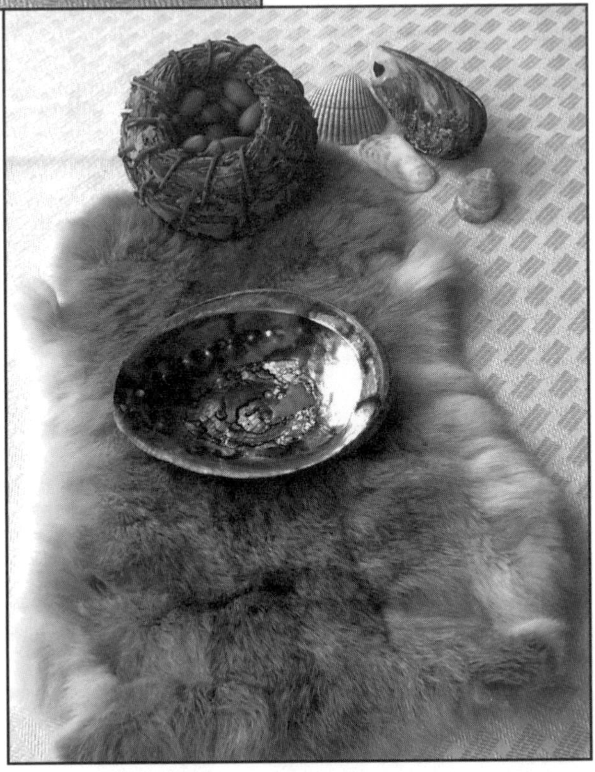

Typical California Indian food: acorns in a willow leaf basket, shellfish and rabbit.
Collection of Mission Dolores

The Franciscans

"The benefits and tranquility I seek for the Indians as well as the mission (Mission San Francisco de Asis) have guided my quill in this appeal. I love the Indians very much and I will feel their misfortunes even more if they are to be treated like this. I repeat, I love them very much, because they have caused me great sorrow, very bad days, many sleepless nights, some tears, and ultimately my shattered health. In return and with good will I dedicate what little health I have left and shall expend it to help them until not one drop of blood is left in my veins. I have relieved them of a thousand burdens that have not been kept secret from your Excellency. I have cared for them for one year to the limit of my strength."

"From a letter of Fray José Mariá Fernández in 1797"

Stained glass windowf St. Francis of Assisi in the Basilica crafted by the Meyer Stained Glass Co.

Collection of Mission Dolores

Statue of St. Francis of Assisi Contemplating the Cross. This statue was placed over the Main Altar of Mission Dolores in 1796.
Collection of Mission Dolores

A Franciscan is a member of a religious community that follows Jesus in the way of Francis of Assisi. Francis found God in everything and worked for a world where there would be peace and everything good for all people. Francis would sing songs about his love of God and how God was praised by all of Creation, even by water and fire. Saint Francis, called "San Francisco de Asís" in Spanish, died in Italy in the year 1226. Fray Junípero Serra founded the first mission in Alta California of San Diego de Alcalá in 1769. In 1776 he sent one of his students and fellow Franciscan from Majorca, Fray Francisco Palóu, to found Mission San Francisco de Asís. Serra's dream was the winning of the hearts and souls of California's First Peoples. He hungered to bring people to the God he worshiped. His vision was not only formed by Spanish culture and Christian morality. Serra had also been a professor in a Franciscan seminary in Majorca, Spain, as was Palóu. Fray Junípero taught the philosophy of Dun Scotus who believed that God is discovered within communities where people live and love each other.

The Franciscan goal was to create Christian societies where God's love would be revealed in the relationships within human communities. The primary focus of the California Missions was the Indians, not only to convert them to Christianity, but also to feed and cloth them. It would be the goal of the Franciscans at the missions to gather native peoples into villages, teach Christianity and European technology and cultural values. They would help establish Spanish law and government and build townships of the Spanish Empire. The Indians would become

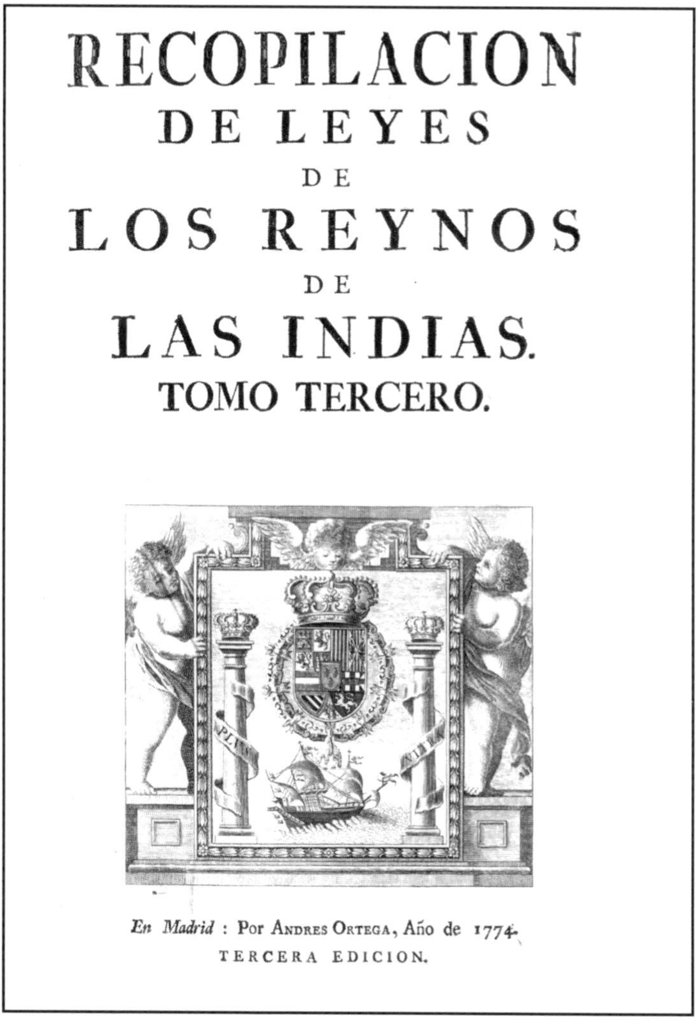
RECOPILACION
DE LEYES
DE
LOS REYNOS
DE
LAS INDIAS.
TOMO TERCERO.

En Madrid : Por ANDRES ORTEGA, Año de 1774.
TERCERA EDICION.

Title page from a 1774 Spanish law book setting out relationships between Indians and the Spanish Empire.
Collection of Mission Dolores

Ink sketch of Mission Dolores as it appeared around 1850.
Collection of the Society of Saint Francis

farmers, ranchers and artisans. Spanish law provided that Indian tribes entering the mission system would have their lands preserved under the management of the mission padres. The intention was to have self-governing pueblos in place within 10 years. Although California's Indians were the primary focus of the padres, the missions would serve important functions for the settlers as well. The soldiers and civilians depended on missions for food and manufactured goods. The missions made loans. Gov. Figueroa said of the California missions in 1834, "Military and civilians depended on missions, (which) made loans, were hostels where travelers and poor received food, lodging, horses, or whatever they wanted free of charge. California missions were the sole source of the prosperity of the territory."

The Soldiers

"The mission of San Francisco, which was founded at the Laguna and Arroyo de los Dolores, a site very beautiful and abundant in water, wood, and stone, is now also completed, and so handsomely built that I can do no less than marvel to

see in so brief a time erected in the face of such a shortage of men a presidio and a mission such as in many years these northern California establishments will not have seen. Now returning to the explorations which I have made of these lands, in which I was accompanied by the reverend fathers, toward the southeast I encountered timber sufficient to build commodious houses, and I saw the land to be well pastured and able to maintain a great number of cattle, and to support no small plantings of the necessary grains. Moreover, I saw that the heathen had burned many patches, which doubtless would produce an abundance of pasturage. In the rest of the explorations which I have made in the vicinity of the mission and the presidio I have found good lands, some large lagoons, little arroyos, and innumerable springs of fresh water which are permanent, although the year has been so short of rain. The Indians in the vicinity of the presidio and mission are of such good disposition that ever since the day when we arrived at this destination they have daily frequented one establishment and the other with such satisfaction on our part that we hope

The first known photograph of Mission Dolores. Dolores Street is a dirt road and some of the friary buildings are still standing. C. 1856.
Collection of Mission Dolores

soon to see harvested the fruit which so Catholic a breast as that of your Excellency desires." [Letter of Lieutenant José Joaquin Moraga reporting the settlement of San Francisco in 1776.]

When we talk about the soldiers who came to Alta California in 1776 sometimes we think of the Spanish Empire soldiers wearing steel helmets and armor, riding great horses, and armed with canons. Perhaps the scene of the Presidio of San Francisco in its founding year of 1776 was something closer to the old Don Quixote de la Mancha on a broken down horse and with a dishpan for a helmet. Some 200 people came on the De Anza party. Of them 33 were soldiers, mostly wearing leather jackets and carrying lances. Most of the party consisted of their wives and children. You might say that the "Conquest" of California was mostly made up of some 123 children and 37 wives and widows. The canons at the Presidio that came later were military "hand-me-downs" from Peru, more than 100 years old.

Bronze statue of King Carlos III given to San Francisco by Spain. King Carlos was monarch of Spain during the time of the expansion of the Spanish Empire into Alta California.
Courtesy of the San Francisco Arts Commission.

Life must have been very hard and uncertain for the soldiers and their families. Many had left their homes in Sonora, Mexico because of a long drought in an otherwise pleasant climate. The families were from different backgrounds. Most were of mixed Spanish, Indian and African descent.

Imagine walking or riding a horse hundreds of miles from your home in Mexico to a country that had only been visited a few times before by people from the Spanish Empire and perhaps full of hostile natives. The boys often assisted the men responsible for several hundred head of cattle and horses. Every time the party stopped you would have to take the saddles and blankets off all of the horses. On arriving at San Francisco, there were no shelters. The people had to build them right away. Of course they had been living in the open for several months on the trail. Still life was probably very exciting and if sometimes dangerous and uncertain. New lands were explored with their Indian peoples, learning about the plants and animals of his

Bronze statue of Captain Juan Bautista de Anza given to San Francisco by Mexico. De Anza, a native of Arizona, was responsible for leading the first settlers from Mexico to San Francisco in 1776.

Courtesy of the San Francisco Arts Commission.

region. Even after the building of the military base called "el Presidio" life was full of hard work. Most of the men were soldiers and were responsible for escorting missionaries into new territories, acting as guards at the missions and taking messages back and forth from the base at Monterey. There were no schools for the children and very few people could read or write. The women were usually responsible for the kitchen gardens, preparing food, sewing, tending the sick and raising the children.

Memorial to 5,000 California Indians buried at Mission Dolores. The figure is that of Blessed Kateri Tekwitha, a Mohawk woman in the process of being made a saint.
Collection of Mission Dolores

Most of the supplies for the soldiers and their families came up by packet ships from San Blas in Mexico once or twice a year. Every thing made from iron had to be imported. Tools, dishes, some clothing, medicines and much more had to be ordered from Mexico. Recent archeological research at El Presidio de San Francisco has given us much information about the daily life of people. By looking at trash pits we know something about their food. The Account Book at Mission San Francisco lists purchases of wheat, corn, lard and beans. We know what their food was like. Meat was very important. Much of their food was in the form of meat stews and served with corn tortillas. Archeologists in 2003 discovered the remains of an adobe house that belonged to the Briones family. Juana Briones was a famous Californio woman who raised food to sell to sailors and acted as a herbalist and doctor. Children would help in chores and of course play games and join in celebrations. The Californio settlers were famous for their fiestas and fandangos which might last for several days. Music, dancing and food would fill the days. The Californio world was mostly soldiers, their families, retired soldiers and later descendants of soldiers. The world of Spanish California was a very small world and it started with soldiers and their families.

These three groups of people: Ohlone, Franciscans and Soldiers and Settlers have different stories about their lives and dreams and the beginnings of San Francisco. One story does not tell us everything. If we leave out a story we lose much and the voice of those people will not be heard saying, "Here is the story of my life. Do not forget me."

View of the Bay of Dolores from a German illustrated newspaper, circa 1865.
Collection of Mission Dolores

CHAPTER 3
Life in Mission Times

The Mission Dolores Slowly Grows

We must not forget that it was the Indians of the California Missions who created these immense agricultural, ranching and manufacturing enterprises. Within one generation the Ohlone, Miwok, Patwin, Wappo and Yokuts peoples of the Bay Area had built several churches and dozens of buildings included housing, workshops, storerooms, granaries, mills, bathhouses and aqueducts. The material progress of those first thirty-five years is astonishing. The Indian population of the mission went from nothing to over 1,000 persons. By 1810 the Indians had almost one thousand horses, over twenty thousand sheep and cattle and were growing over 8,500 bushels of wheat, barley, corn, beans, peas every year.

This was not all. The Indians were building their town and everything necessary for it. Within twenty-five years they had built several church buildings with living quarters for the padres, corrals for horses and mules, a 3,025 foot long aqueduct and other irrigation projects. Also, an agricultural station of Mission San Francisco, called the *Asistencia of San Pedro y San Pablo* was constructed at present day San Mateo, some 19 miles south of Mission San Francisco. As well, storehouses, orchards, warehouses, mills, a bathhouse and all the buildings necessary for trades such as leather working, weaving, tanning, black smithing, tile making and over sixty-five homes for neophyte families. The only surviving building from the mission era is the present Mission Dolores church.

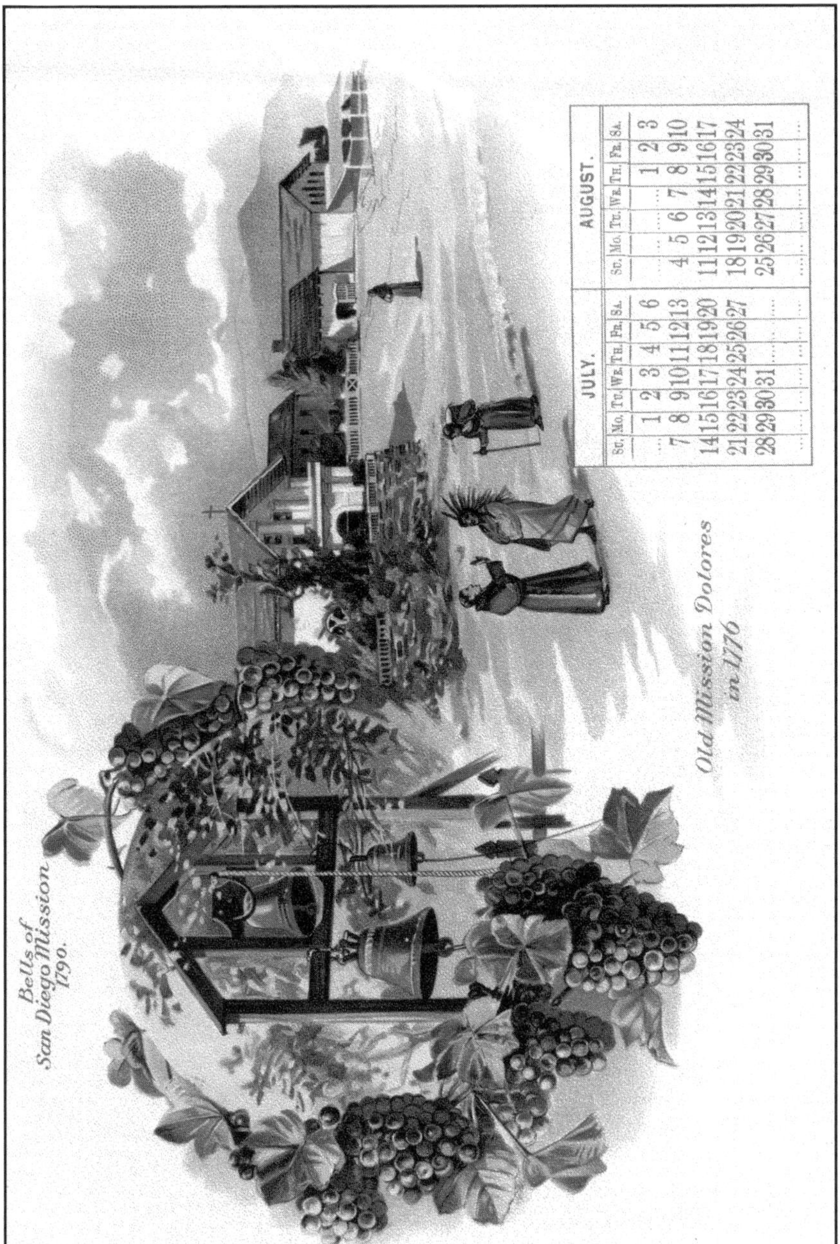
Bells of San Diego Mission 1790.
Old Mission Dolores in 1776
JULY.
Su. Mo. Tu. We. Th. Fr. Sa.
1 2 3 4 5 6
7 8 9 10 11 12 13
14 15 16 17 18 19 20
21 22 23 24 25 26 27
28 29 30 31
AUGUST.
Su. Mo. Tu. We. Th. Fr. Sa.
1 2 3
4 5 6 7 8 9 10
11 12 13 14 15 16 17
18 19 20 21 22 23 24
25 26 27 28 29 30 31

Mission Dolores, looking towards San Francisco - 1850.
Sketch by William H. Dougal.
Bancroft Library, University of California at Berkeley

The labor, creativity and skills of the Indians of California built an astonishingly complex ranching, agricultural and manufacturing enterprise at Mission Dolores and the other missions of California. While the process of conversion to Christianity was mostly voluntary, once baptized an Indian became the child of the mission and subject to what to our modern eyes must appear to be oppressive and controlling in the extreme. It is unclear if the neophytes understood the implications of a Baptism after a very brief teaching. The new Christians would become the legal wards of the Franciscans and have most of their life influenced, governed and controlled by the padres and their alcaldes. Setbacks at Mission Dolores included a mass exodus of 280 people in the Summer of 1795 due to the "Three *Muchos*:" too much work, too much

(Picture on the left) A calendar for 1911 showing a Franciscan padre welcoming an Indian incorrectly shown as a member of a Great Plains nation.
Collection of Mission Dolores

punishment and too much hunger. Periodic epidemics of measles, smallpox, diphtheria and other diseases drastically reduced mission populations. Franciscans sometimes quarreled with each other and wrote letters of complaint to their superiors about the Indians, the soldiers and sometimes each other. In many ways, this story of politics and human struggle and debate could be a story we could read in today's newspaper or experience in our own homes or workplaces.

Wood block print of Mission Dolores from 1851 from a Gold Rush era newspaper.
Collection of Mission Dolores

What was life like in the world of the California Missions during their heyday? Let us imagine a journey from the capital of Alta California in Montery to San Francisco in 1820. Monterey had a Presidio, Customs House and was the seat of government. It would not be a three hour drive along a freeway. You would have been walking on tired feet, jolted on horseback or shaken in a cart without springs *(carreta)* along a dirt track grandly called, The Royal Road "*el Camino Real.*" Nineteen miles before you arrived at Mission San Francisco you would have been on its land. Perhaps you would have stopped for the night at the Asistencia de San Pedro y Paulo. This assisting mission and the principal farmsteads of

Full size replica of a Spanish carreta, used to move people and goods along El Camino Real in Mission times. Santa Barbara Presidio
Collection of Mission Dolores

Mission Dolores were in what is now San Mateo. It contained a field some 8,250 feet in length and 30 feet in width bounded by willow trees. In addition to wheat, beans, peas, maize and barley, an orchard contained peaches, quinces and grapes. There was a chapel, housing for the workers and various farm buildings. The Sanchez Adobe in Pacifica is on the site of the Old Mission farm. Continuing on your journey you would have passed by huge herds of cattle grazing in the southern part of what is now San Francisco and passing mission horses grazing inside a four foot high stone enclosure on Potrero Hill, all of which were part of the Mission. At last you would come to the *Laguna y Arroyo de Nuestra Senora de Los Dolores.* (The Lake and Creek of Our Lady of Sorrows). Dolores Creek is now under 18th Street and still occasionally overflows the sewer openings at 18th and Dolores Streets in the rainy season. The lagoon roughly extended from Guerrero to Capp Streets and 15th to 19th Streets. Crossing Dolores Creek you would finally arrive to Mission San Francisco de Asís and the Pueblo Dolores. In 1815 Pueblo Dolores would have had about 700 people in residence making it larger than the Mexican towns of Los Angeles, San Jose

This reredos was brought from Mexico by ship in 1796 and is the oldest of its kind still in its original place in California. Hidden behind the reredos is a mural believed to have been painted by Indian artists in 1791.
Collection of Mission Dolores

and Branciforte in Alta California. The mission quadrangle containing the Mission church seen today on the south, the friary on the east and workshops and storerooms on the north and west had been complete for about two decades. Other buildings in the village included a granary, a home for the Indian alcalde or majordomo, a residence for unmarried women (*monjério*), about 85 homes of adobe and tile for the neophytes, a barracks for the soldiers, mill, storerooms, community bath, and other buildings for industries of weaving, black smithing, leather working, cooking, etc., etc. There

These statues and the reredos holding them were brought from Mexico by ship in 1810. They may be some of the last items brought to Northern California on the military supply ships before they ceased operation due to the Mexican War of Indpendence that began in 1810.

Collection of Mission Dolores

were several aqueducts including one a mile long leading to pasture lands and one over 3,000 feet in length bringing water from a spring in what is now Duboce Park. A fruit orchard surrounded by an adobe wall was across El Camino Real on what is now Notre Dame Plaza.

The church would have been little different from what we see today at Mission Dolores. Built at ground level (Dolores Street was graded and lowered in the 1890s), we would enter into a building with a dirt floor, no pews, and more painted wall decoration than is currently visible (alas, whitewashed some 50 years ago). Aside from the electric lighting, it would appear much as you see it today. The side altars had only recently come up from Mexico in 1810, perhaps one of the last shipments on the royal packet ships supplying Alta California. This would have Mission Dolores at the height of its

Interior of Mission Dolores. The Great Altar was placed in 1796, while the two side altars were placed in 1810. The chevron or zigzag pattern on the ceiling was originally painted in 1791 by Indian artists and may represent Indian designs used in basket work or body decoration.

Collection of Mission Dolores

prosperity and in the last years of the Spanish Empire in Alta California.

The primary inhabitants of the missions were the Indian peoples. To give you an idea of the ethnic proportions of the time, the first 50 years of burial records at Mission Dolores (1776-1826) show that of the first 5,154 burials only some 132 were not Indians. The California Missions were the greatest commercial, agricultural, ranching and manufacturing enterprises seen in California in 12,000 years of human habitation. It is estimated that over 50 different crafts, arts and enterprises were carried out at Mission Dolores. Some, such as teaching and music, continue to this day. Fray Francisco Palóu, the first pastor at Mission Dolores, has been called California's first historian and his book about California was written at Mission San Francisco. The writing of history is still a craft practiced today at Mission Dolores.

The Indians owned the means of production, lived and worked collectively and shared in the profits. It is estimated that 90% of the

Replica of Mexican "Liberty Bell" in Dolores Park. The war for Mexican Independence began in the parish of Dolores in Mexico.
Courtesy of the San Francisco Arts Commission.

Statue of Padre Miguel Hildalgo in Dolores Park. Hildalgo began the war for Mexican Independence by ringing the bell of the parish church of Dolores in Mexico.
Courtesy of the San Francisco Arts Commission.

productive output of the missions was put back into the mission system. Some Indians occasionally performed work for the Presidio and received wages. The account books of Mission Dolores record purchases of luxury imported goods, such as chocolate and silk by Indians. However, there was very little money in circulation in California and most Indians received only the basic necessities of life such as clothing, shelter and food. Significant investments were made in tools and the decoration of the Mission church.

It is difficult for us in the urbanized San Francisco of today to imagine life in Mission Dolores in its final years. The holdings of the mission included most of present day San Francisco, east to Alameda and south to San Mateo. At its height in 1812 the Indian population of Mission Dolores was about 1,224 persons. In contrast, the non-Indian population of San Francisco in 1815 was a mere 131 persons. What is especially difficult for us to imagine is life under fairly strict external controls. Indians rose at dawn for

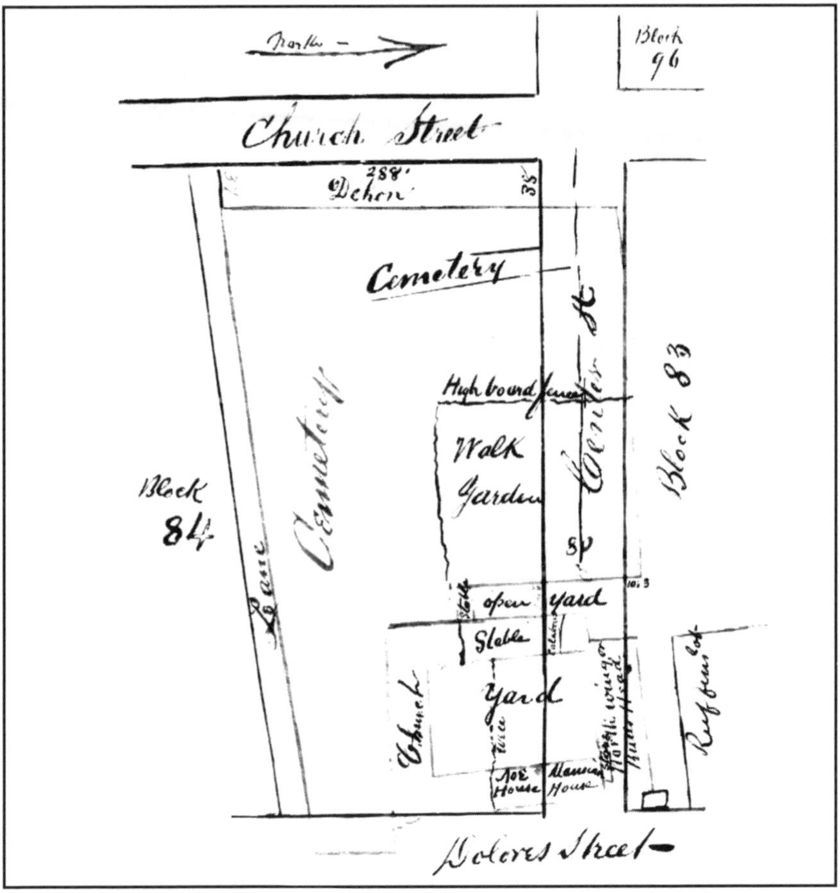

A hand drawn block map of Mission Dolores around 1860. 16th Street is called "Center Street" and is not yet cut through to join Church and Dolores Streets.
Collection of Mission Dolores

morning prayers and instruction followed by a first meal of *atole*, a grain porridge. After breakfast the men and boys would work in workshops, fields and ranches. Women would work on food preparation, child care and textile manufacture. Work ceased at Noon and a meal of *posolera,* a meat, vegetable and grain stew followed after prayers. Work resumed at 2:00 p.m. and continued until 5:00 p.m. More prayers followed until supper was served at 6:00 p.m. consisting of more *atole*. Free time followed until 8:00 p.m. It was expected that an adobe brick maker could make 28 bricks in one six hour work day. A neophyte could not leave the Mission without permission. There were frequent days off for religious fiestas. A remarkable series of drawings of life at Mission Dolores was prepared by the Russian artist Louis Choris of the Russian ship *Rurik* in 1816 and shows Indians at Mission Dolores performing a stick game and playing drums and rattle sticks. Another drawing shows gambling and still more sketches document clothing and the faces of those Indians living in Pueblo Dolores during this period.

The most important industries of the people of the mission were ranching, agriculture and manufacturing. Men and boys might be responsible for raising the thousands of cattle, horses and mules. In addition to the farms there were fruit orchards. Much of the clothing at the mission was woven from the wool of thousands of sheep. It is said that the women of the mission had twenty looms to produce cloth.

Mission era chair and the Ohlone candle stick which has stood in the sanctuary of Mission Dolores for two centuries.

Collection of Mission Dolores.

Mission Dolores was less productive than other missions, primarily due to the climate of the northern San Francisco peninsula. However, the output was sufficient to supply a good sized village. Meals at Mis-

Loom typical of ones used by California Mission Indians. This is a model on display at el Presidio de Santa Barbara.

sion Dolores were largely communal. George von Langsdorff, a German scientist on the Russian sponsored Rezanov expedition, who visited Mission Dolores, in 1806 described the meals of the neophytes as about three pints per person per meal and it appeared to him "...incomprehensible how any one could three times a day eat so large a portion of such nourishing food." Forty to fifty cattle were slaughtered every week to supply meat for some 800-1,200 people. Cow bones and teeth have been discovered at Mission Dolores and under the street during recent sewer and conduit construction and repair. This diet was also supplemented by shellfish, fish, acorns, seeds and other foods hunted and harvested by the Indians.

Occasionally agricultural surplus would be sold. There is an amusing report from 1821 wherein Governor Pablo de Solá found the price of merchandise being sold by the Russian merchant ship *Buldakoff* so exorbitant that he asked the Franciscans to raise the price of the wheat being sold to the Russian colony. Sola went on to marvel that Mission Dolores had no wheat to sell previously to the Presidio, but now suddenly had wheat for sale to foreigners when the price was right. The Franciscan vow of poverty apparently did not prevent them from being shrewd businessmen!

Hides of cattle were processed into leather and sold to New England merchants. These sales were the principal source of coin money during the period and hides were sometimes called "California dollars." Fat was processed into tallow. Craftspeople at the mission produced saddles, shoes and other things made of leather.

At its peak Mission San Francisco de Asís had some 1100 Ohlone, Miwok, Wappo, Patwin and Yokuts peoples associated with the Mission. Of the hundreds of people living in the pueblo, only two were Spanish (the Franciscan padres), three to five were Mexican soldiers of mixed ancestry and the rest were Indians. The Indians built the mission church, the barns, warehouses, ranches and aqueducts. It is they who carried out the dozens of crafts and operated the ranches and farms. Of the first 5,000 people buried in the mission cemetery, all but 200 were Indian. Recent research indicates that 90% of the economic output of the mission Indians went back into support the mission enterprises, i.e., the missions were virtually entirely supported by Indian productivity and they received the products of their labor back in food, clothing, shelter and the decoration of their church. Indian leadership included elections for their Alcaldes (mayors) in 1779 and the supervisors in charge of various works. Was Mission San Francisco de Asís a Spanish Mission or was it an Indian town? The question does not answer easily. In the same way we as people of the 21st century have difficulty making sense of the expansion of empires, forced labor and physical punishment. The question of how the Indians were treated in the California Missions occupied people of the 18th and 19th centuries as well. The quote from Fray José María Fernández is taken from a letter he wrote in June 1797 to Governor Diego de Borica protesting the sending of Indians to the East Bay to bring back fugitive Indians to Mission Dolores. Gov. Borica had expressly forbidden such tactics and Fernández was sent back to Mexico City by his Franciscan superiors for protesting the aggressive tactics of his fellow Franciscan missionaries and taking sides with the civil government and the Indian people intrusted to his care. His fellow Franciscans believed they were doing the best they could for the Indians by bringing them back to Mission Dolores after they had fled. My personal view is that the missions operated with the best of intentions and with nearly the worst of results. To this day the California Missions represent pride and pain, memory and faith for the First Peoples who built and lived in these twenty-one missions of Alta California.

The Last Supper set in an architectural fantasy. This huge canvas was painted locally around 1815. Behind this canvas are hidden 1791 Indian designs painted on the wall of the mission.

Collection of Mission Dolores

CHAPTER 4
Changing Times

Revolution, War, and California

On the morning of September 16, 1810 a bell was rung in Dolores. Not our Mission Dolores, in fact Mission San Francisco de Asís was not to be called Mission Dolores for another 15 years. In the town of Dolores in the state of Guanajunto Father Miguel Hildago y Castilla rang a bell to signal the beginning of the Mexican War of Independence. A replica of the bell and a statue of Father Hidalgo stand in Dolores Park today. Echos of that bell were to be heard as far away as Alta California and that bell would become a tolling bell as the Franciscan Missions entered both their greatest years of prosperity and the beginning of forces which would result in their closure. Soon the begrudging support of the military and retired military population of California by the missions would became a source of resentment for the Californios who were forced to come begging to the Franciscans with sombrero in hand. Adelbert von Chamisso visited San Francisco in 1816 with the Russian ship Rurik and reported that while the missions had an abundance of food, soldiers of the presidios had not eaten bread in years and what few supplies they had received from the Franciscans were only provided after the signing of promissory notes. Eventually the tables would be turned and it would be the Franciscans who would be at the mercy of the military and civil government. The effect of the revolution was catastrophic on the military of Alta California. The packet ships bringing supplies from Mexico and the flow of money and credit ceased. Economic stagnation set in, commerce was non-

1849 newspaper drawing of Mission Dolores and the remains of the Indian village at the time of the Gold Rush.
Library of Congress - Historic American Buildings Survey

existent and the military and civilian population outside the missions were reduced to near subsistence level. There was no pay for the troops from 1810. Pressure was put on the missions to either surrender land to the Mexican settlers or support the government by gifts of food and manufactured products.

The process of removing the material, economic and commercial operations (sometimes called temporalities) of the missions from the control of the Franciscans is called "secularization." The missions were not intended to be permanent organizations. The plan was for the Indian villages surrounding the missions to be turned into self-governing townships within ten years of their establishment. This was a complete failure, particularly at Mission Dolores. The Spanish Empire "Law of the Indies" specified that Indian tribes converting to Christianity would have their tribal lands preserved intact. As practically every tribe of California coastal Indian, from San Diego to San Francisco, had entered the mission system by 1810. There was very little land left for settlement by retiring military personnel. Due to Franciscan protests about utilization of Indian land, the Presidio of San Francisco was forced to pasture its cattle in distant Monterey after 1791. The attitude of the Californios to the missions was a spectrum from liberal ideas on the dignity and emancipation of Indians and participation in society by all races and classes to personal fears that the settlers of California had been left outside access to the primary resource of land to simple greed in desiring to appropriate the resources of the missions and utilization of Indian labor. Many Californios believed that the

Stereographic view of Mission Dolores published by S&L. c. 1860s. Part of the old friary has been turned into a saloon called The Mansion House.
Collection of Mission Dolores

Stereographic view of Mission Dolores published by Watkin. c. 1860s
Collection of Mission Dolores

missions were a form of slavery and incompatible with the new Mexican constitution. The first moves towards secularization began in 1813. On November 3, 1834 Governor Figueroa published a decree of the Territorial Deputation which ordered the missionaries to be made into curates of parishes and the vast mission holdings and enterprises to be given over to administrators appointed by the government. Mission Dolores, due to its relatively small size and unimportance, was made a second class curacy and its curate assigned a salary of $1,000 per year or 1/3 less than a first class curacy. In 1834 the lands and possessions of Mission Dolores were confiscated and handed over for management to Commissioner José Joaquin Estudillo. In September 1835 the village surrounding the mission was recognized as Pueblo de Dolores. The church holdings were restricted to the church building, buildings occupied by the

Mission Dolores in the 1860s.
Collection of Mission Dolores

The centennial of Mission Dolores and the dedication of the new parish church on the right. Notice the decorations on the church and the dirt road. 1876. The road was not paved until 1900. *Collection of Mission Dolores*

clergy, cemetery, orchard and contents. The rest was theoretically to be turned over to the Indian neophytes. However, within five years the Indian population of the former Mission Dolores was reduced to about 50 persons, mostly resident on former Mission Dolores holdings in San Mateo. In 1842 a petition was made by the eight remaining Indians of San Francisco sadly describing

Stereographic view of Mission Dolores. c. 1860s.
Collection of Mission Dolores

Boys from Mission Dolores school in front of the Old Mission. Note the church is at ground level. Dolores Street would not be graded and paved until 1900. c. 1880.
Collection of Mission Dolores

their poverty, hunger, lack of property and means of support, advanced age and fatigue from a lifetime of labor. Governor Pio Pico issued a warning to the remaining Indians that if they did not return to Pueblo Dolores their land would be sold. The Indians failed to return or respond and on October 28, 1845 Pico decreed the missions finally closed. A subsequent grant of the land was made on February 10, 1846 because the Indians had allegedly abandoned the property. The U.S. Supreme Court later set aside the grant as fraudulent. By then, it was too late for the Indians who had scattered, died or been absorbed into the Mexican population.

The last Franciscan missionary to serve at Mission Dolores was Padre José Real . In 1845 he departed Mission Dolores to take up residence at Mission Santa Clara. What few Indians remained drifted away to either beg or act as servants or labor for ranches held by the now land wealthy Mexicans. After the American seizure of California in 1846 the Land Commission began to hold hearings on the various land claims. On March 3, 1858 President James Buchanan confirmed the return of land and property constituting the former Mission Dolores to the Roman Catholic Archbishop of San Francisco, James S. Alemany, O.P. From a holding of some 130 miles in circumference, Mission Dolores was reduced to just over the 4 acres situated at 16th and Dolores Streets. Within another 20 years most of the adobe buildings making up the mission complex and Pueblo Dolores were gone.

The period 1835 to 1846 was an uncertain time for the now secularized missions of Alta California. On July 8, 1846 Captain John B. Montgomery of the American warship *Portsmouth*,

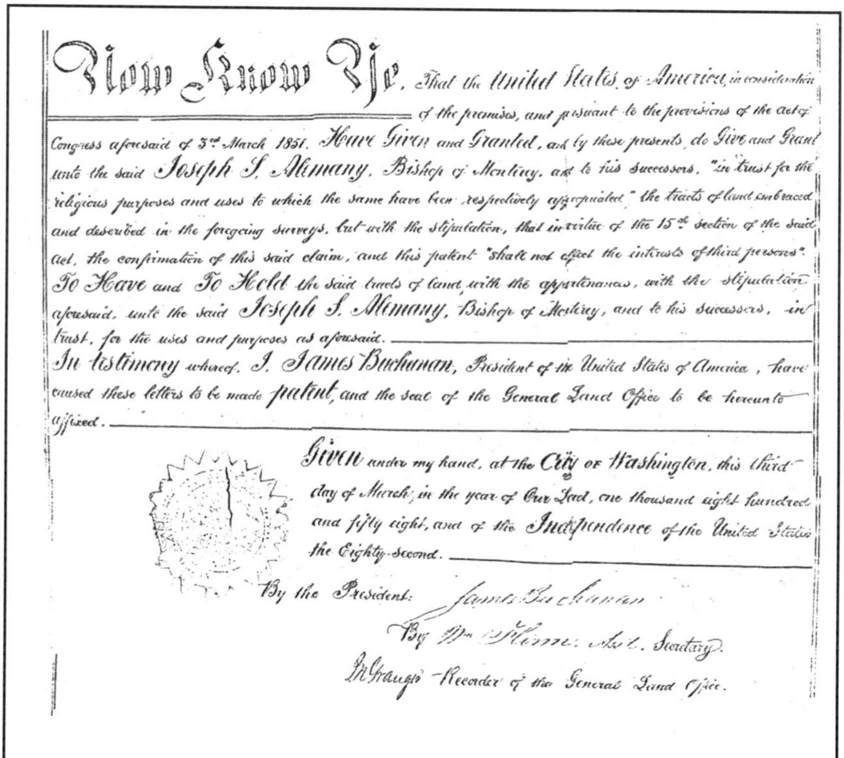
Now Know Ye, That the United States of America, in consideration of the premises, and pursuant to the provisions of the act of Congress aforesaid of 3rd March 1851, Have Given and Granted, and by these presents, do Give and Grant unto the said Joseph S. Alemany, Bishop of Monterey, and to his successors, "in trust for the religious purposes and uses to which the same have been respectively appropriated," the tracts of land embraced and described in the foregoing surveys, but with the stipulation, that in virtue of the 15th section of the said act, the confirmation of this said claim, and this patent "shall not affect the interests of third persons". To Have and To Hold the said tracts of land, with the appurtenances, with the stipulation aforesaid, unto the said Joseph S. Alemany, Bishop of Monterey, and to his successors, in trust, for the uses and purposes as aforesaid.

In testimony whereof, I, James Buchanan, President of the United States of America, have caused these letters to be made patent, and the seal of the General Land Office to be hereunto affixed.

Given under my hand, at the City of Washington, this third day of March, in the year of Our Lord, one thousand eight hundred and fifty eight, and of the Independence of the United States the Eighty-second.

By the President: James Buchanan

By Wm. [illegible] Asst. Secretary.

[illegible] Recorder of the General Land Office.

Land Grant 1856 signed by President James Buchanan confirming ownership of Mission Dolores to Archbishop James S. Alemany after the American acquisition of California from Mexico.

Collection of the Archdiocese of San Francisco.

Circa 1900. The Old Mission and the 1876 brick parish church.
Collection of Mission Dolores

Circa 1880 view of Mission Dolores.
Collection of Mission Dolores

raised the Stars and Stripes over San Francisco and claimed California for the Unites States of America. This was confirmed by the Treaty of Guadalupe Hildalgo on February 2, 1848. The area around Mission Dolores was a mostly Spanish area in contrast to the area around the harbor (called Yerba Buena) which was mostly American. Most of the buildings in the compound of Mission Dolores were taken over for secular purposes. The building of two plank roads from Yerba Buena to the Mission District in the 1850s allowed easy access to what became an entertainment district. Bull and bear fights, gambling, drinking, and other entertainments became a feature of the place, although the mission church continued as a place of prayer. Some of the buildings were turned into a hospital, German brewery, saloons, gambling hall, etc. The acquisition of Alta California by the United States of America began an investigation into the land claims asserted by the Mexicans. Most of these claims had been carved out of what had previously been mission holdings. Much of the immediate land of the mission became part of Rancho San Miguel, owned by the Noe family. On March 3, 1851, President James Buchanan confirmed some four acres of the original immense holdings of Mission Dolores to Bishop Alemany.

On March 18, 1848, one of San Francisco's most prominent citizens, William Alexander Leidesdorff, died and was laid to rest inside the mission church. Most of San Francisco's population of some 400 were said to have attended the burial. Within two years the population had grown to more than 25,000. Many of the Argonauts were Irish, French, and German Roman Catholics and the burial registers show a change from predominately Spanish names to Irish. San Francisco was definitely the Queen of All the Golden West and attracted many colorful and outrageous characters. On July 2, 1853, the notorious "Spanish Dancer," Lola Montez was married at Mission Dolores. After a scandalous affair with King Ludwig I of Bavaria brought down his government, Ms. Montez ended up in California. The marriage register is still preserved at Mission Dolores and Montez apparently lied about her age, religion and prior marital status. Ah! show business! In the cemetery are buried several victims of the Vigilantes. In a time of rough and ready justice at the hands of the Committee of Vigilance, three men were executed for shooting the editor of a newspaper, dueling and ballot box stuffing.

In honor of the centennial of San Francisco in 1876 and to accommodate a growing population, Mission Dolores dedicated a new red brick Victorian neo-gothic church. The erection of a modern church next door to the old mission allowed for the adobe church and its Spanish era art to be preserved, or at least largely forgotten by many except as a relic of the past.

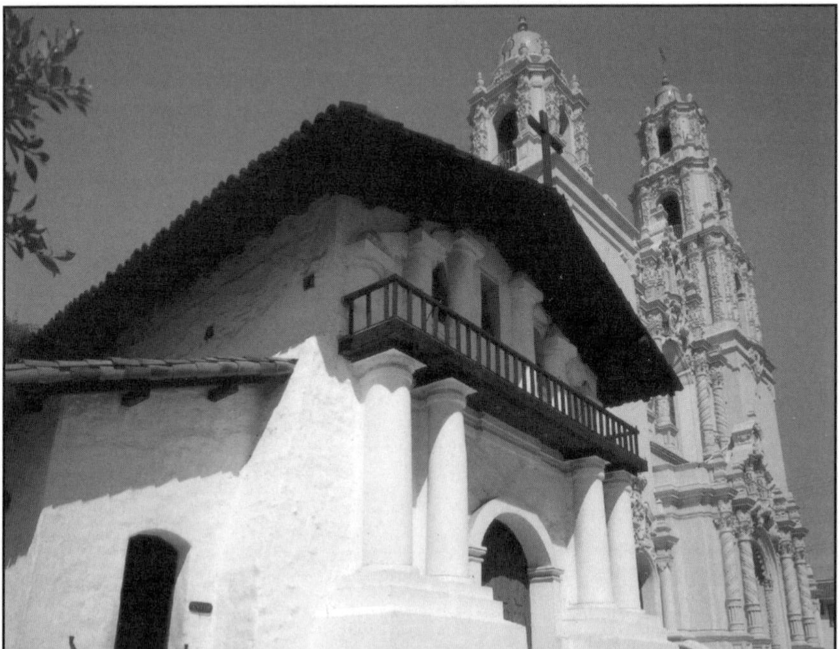

Mission Dolores and Basilica today.
Collection of Mission Dolores

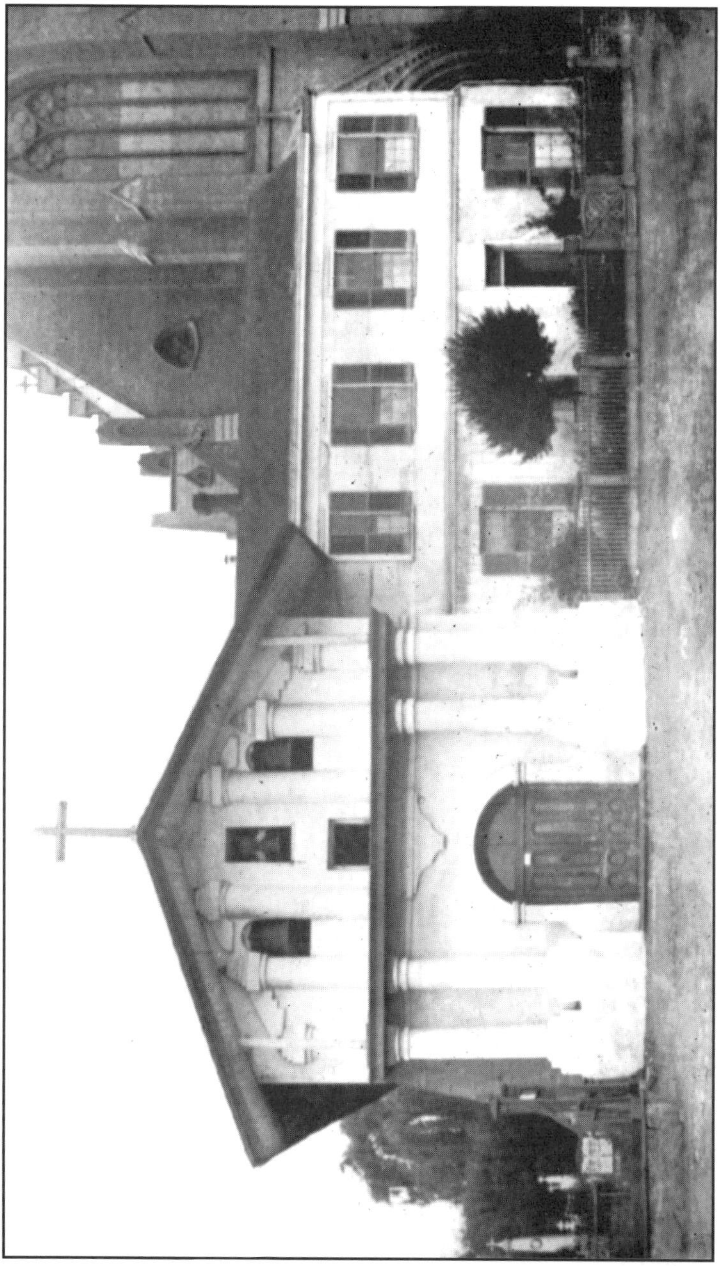

A rare photograph from a glass plate negative of the Mission Dolores, taken in the 1870s.
Collection of Mission Dolores

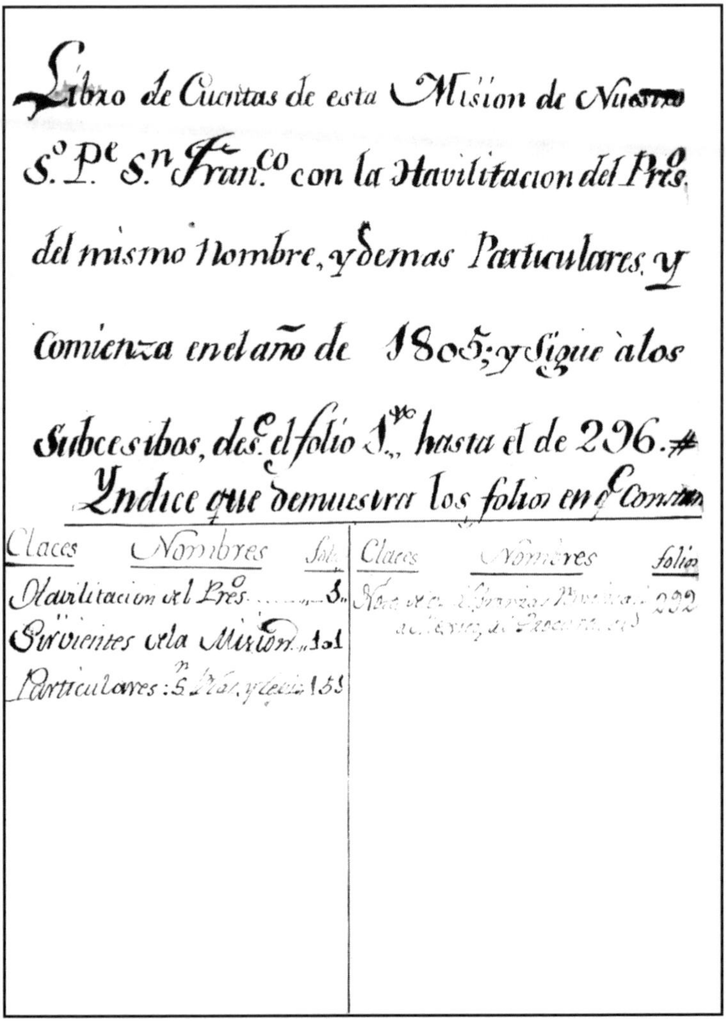

Libro de Cuentas de esta Mision de Nuestro S.o P.e S.n Fran.co con la Havilitacion del Pres.o del mismo Nombre, y demas Particulares, y Comienza en el año de 1805; y Sigue à los Subcesibos, des.e el folio 1.o hasta el de 296. #

Yndice que demuestra los folios en q.e Comien...

Claces	Nombres	fol.	Claces	Nombres	folio
Havilitacion del Pres.o		3	[illegible]		292
Sirvientes de la Mision		101			
Particulares: S.n Mar. y [illegible]		155			

Title page from the Account Book of Mission Dolores. This book detailed harvests, livestock and sales of supplies to Indian and military families and the Russians at Fort Ross. This is the only such account book in the California Missions that continues into the Mexican Period (1810-1846).

Collection of Mission Dolores

CHAPTER 5
Disaster and Recovery

Queen of All the Golden West

The 20th century found San Francisco to be truly the "Queen of All the Golden West." Gold and silver from the mines poured into her banks. Farmlands opened up and the old forests of Redwood trees supplied timber. Thousands of ships entered her harbor carrying the wealth of the world and new settlers. Colleges, libraries and theaters opened up bringing in the culture of the East Coast and Europe. Oscar Wilde joked that anyone who went missing was reported to have been seen in San Francisco. On April 18, 1906, a major earthquake that created fires struck San Francisco. In an effort to save Mission Dolores from destruction, firefighters dynamited the Convent and School of Notre Dame across the street from the mission church. Later this was thought to have been unnecessary. While the original adobe church survived, the 1876 red brick church was severely damaged and torn down. Some 23 square blocks of the 46 square blocks comprising the parish of Mission Dolores were destroyed on April 18-20, 1906. Even in the face of such destruction San Franciscans were still proud and determined to rebuild our city.

One of the many stories of courage and determination following the Earthquake and Fire of 1906 is the story of the women of San Francisco and especially Mission Dolores. In 1983 I was living on a lot in San Francisco that had two small cottages. My neighbor in front was the redoubtable local historian, Jane Cryan. She

1906 An amateur photograph of the destruction of the '1876 brick parish church of Mission Dolores.
Collection of Mission Dolores

1906 People gathered at Mission Dolores after the Great Earthquake and Fire. Ruins of 1876 brick church on right.
Collection of Mission Dolores

The temporary parish church at Mission Dolores after the parish church was destroyed by the Great Earthquake and Fire. c. 1915.
Collection of Mission Dolores

discovered that these cottages had a story of recovery and suffering. Most of the people who died as a result of the 1906 disaster were victims of pneumonia and other illness caught due to the loss of housing. Some 25% of San Francisco's housing was destroyed in those horrible days of April 18, 19 and 20, 1906. In order to house the thousands of now homeless working class families, the U.S. Army undertook to construct 5,000 one room cottages set up in parks around San Francisco. Photos of the time show determined looking women, cooking and washing in the open and setting up schools. It took on a personal meaning for me when Jane Cryan determined that we were living in what was then two of the remaining 44 "Earthquake Cottages." The history of these "Refugee Shacks" is largely forgotten, but Cryan's research found that women of the time, who were still denied the vote, demanded better conditions for their families. They were led by a formidable Irish-American woman, Mary Kelly, with her rallying cry, "We will not be

Christian Mothers Union at Mission Dolores, June 11, 1916.
These are the women who rebuilt San Francisco.
Collection of Mission Dolores

treated like imbeciles!" No doubt she was a terror to politicians of her time and a model for San Francisco local politics today. These same women were the children of Irish immigrants of the Gold Rush who had built the new parish church of Mission Dolores in 1876 and the Mission Dolores grammar school for boys and the remarkable Notre Dame Academy giving grade and high school education to girls across the street from Mission Dolores. The parish church was

Early 20th century lace with a butterfly pattern used as an altar hanging. This was probably made by an Irish-American woman of the parish of Mission Dolores. The butterfly is a symbol of the resurrection of Christ.
Collection of Mission Dolores

ruined in the Earthquake and the Notre Dame Academy was dynamited to prevent the spread of the fire to the old mission church. I discovered two reminders of their stories at Mission Dolores. One is a photo of the Christian Mothers Union of 1910 at Mission Dolores. Believe it: these are the women who rebuilt the parish of Mission Dolores and the City of San Francisco. The other reminder was some of their handiwork. Irish women had a reputation for skilled needle work and especially lace and crochet work. Women of Mission Dolores decorated the altars of the new church with altar cloths made of linen and decorated with yards of hand made lace and crochet. One particularly personal touch was a delicate lace hanging containing the shamrocks of Ireland. This not only a reminder of the craftswoman's love of her parish and ethnic pride. It was a reminder that her family had struggled from being the despised "Shanty Irish" to the respectable middle class "Lace Curtain Irish." These delicate threads by the nameless and nearly forgotten women of Mission Dolores who survived the 1906 Calamity tell a story of extraordinary heroism in ordinary lives.

Some San Franciscans boasted that even after the disaster San Francisco displayed the finest ruins in the world. A temporary church for the people of Mission Dolores was erected along 16th Street. The Old Adobe Church was not neglected and noted San Francisco architect Willis Polk supervised a sensitive retrofitting and restoration of the mission church in 1917. Foundations for a new parish church of steel and concrete were laid in 1913 and the first Mass was held on Christmas Day 1918. Architects Frank T. Shea and John O. Lofquist designed the new parish church in a mixed Mexican Baroque/Moorish style and of concrete and steel to withstand earthquakes.

Decoration of the new church continued for another 15 years and included much Baroque Mexican architectural embellishment. This work, under the direction of architect Henry Minton, was undertaken for the celebration of San Francisco's sesquicentennial in 1926. Particularly noteworthy are the interior mosaics and stained glass windows depicting the 21 Franciscan missions of Alta California executed by the Meyer

Company of Munich. Considerable care went into the design of the art and an amusing series of letters between the Meyer Company and the pastor still exists. Apparently the pastor overruled the artist several times and then later didn't like the result. The artist complained that every window had been redesigned once or twice and that the devalued American dollar made the entire project a "sour deficit." The last of the stained glass windows were installed in 1960, thus completing forty-four years of recovery from the Biggest of Big Ones and no doubt with a sigh of relief by the Meyer Company.

A rare photo of the new parish church before the towers were modified in 1926. C. 1920.

Collection of Mission Dolores

World War II saw many changes in the parish. Many of its people went off to fight, build ships or otherwise support

World War II Merchant Marine Tanker Ship, the SS Mission Dolores.
Courtesy of the Merchant Marines Ships Message and Picture Exchange.

the war effort. Two supply ships were built in Bay Area shipyards were named after the mission, the S.S. Mission Dolores and the S.S. Mission San Francisco.

Its Irish population relocated, and increasingly the parish served a largely Latin American population. On February 8, 1952, Pope Pius XII raised the church to the honor of a Minor Basilica. Mission Dolores became the first church designated a basilica west of the Mississippi River and only the fourth Catholic church in the United States to be so honored at that time. On September 17, 1987, Pope John Paul II became the first reigning Roman Pontiff to visit San Francisco and pray at the Basilica. Particularly memorable and moving was his embracing of a child with AIDS. Another earthquake in 1989 occasioned a major campaign for retrofitting, strengthening and conservation.

The cemetery and the artwork of the old mission church were restored to period appearance in 1995. Today Mission Dolores looks much as it did in 1810.

In 1987 Pope John Paul II visited Mission Dolores and a boy with AIDS spontaneously hugged the Pope.
Collection of Mission Dolores.

Mission Dolores in between 1900 - 1906.

Paragon Agency collection

CHAPTER 6
A Mission in a Modern World

Art, Artifact, Architecture and the Imagination

When we think of the California Missions we think of white washed adobe walls, with red tile roofs and Spanish religious decorations. The missions are that; they are also much more. The art, artifacts and architecture we see are the work of people who imagined, created and labored. If the City of San Francisco is the Gift of Saint Francis, the Mission Dolores we see today is the gift of thousands of people who have worked, and prayed and given of their talent and treasure.

The Old Mission Church

There is something bread-like about adobe bricks. They are usually made with mud, straw, clay and manure, formed by hand into molds and then baked in the sun. There is also a spiritual dimension to adobe. Being formed by hand, the bricks contain minute traces of sweat and flakes of skin. These bricks were formed by Indian artisans and there creation contains a part of their physical bodies that remains today. Using our imagination, we can think of ourselves as being surround by those artisans of the late 18th century when we sit in the adobe church.

The mission church we see today is a rectangular adobe building — 114 feet long, 22 feet wide, and 21 feet high from floor to ceiling. The walls are four feet thick, except for the walls facing Dolores Street, which are ten feet thick. It is thought that the mud for the adobe was taken from the banks of Dolores Creek about where Dolores and Dorland Streets are today. The foundations are four feet wide and four feet deep and said to be of stones quarried from Mint Hill.

In the front wall (façada) of the mission are three niches containing the three original bells brought up from Mexico in the 1790s. The names of the bells, from south to north are San Martin, San Francisco and San Jose. Two of the bells are cracked, but they are still rung, most often by visiting school children under the direction of watchful docents. The central bell is in its original wooden stocks secured by rawhide.

A view of Mission Dolores with the El Camino Real Bell in front. c. 1930.
Collection of Mission Dolores

Many of the roof tiles are the originals made on site in 1794. Mission Dolores is particularly famed for its artwork. Most of the paintings were imported from Mexico before the Revolution of 1810. The principal ornaments are the altars, statues and reredos. The principal altar was brought by ship from Mexico in 1796, while the two side altars followed in 1810.

The U.S. Department of the Interior in its Historic American Buildings Survey of 1936 said of the interior decoration, *"It is a most extraordinary piece of Spanish Baroque decorative art, possibly without equal in North America outside of Mexico."* The principal altar is fashioned in Baroque taste, while the side altars reflect an Enlightenment period taste with a more severe neoclassical style. Also notable are the ceiling rafters decorated in an Ohlone motif of ochre, white, red, and blue/gray colored chevrons.

Comparisons have been made to similar motifs in Ohlone basket work. The holy water fonts at the back of the church are Chinese plates brought to California on the Manila Galleons in the 18th

Chinese plate brought from the Philippine Islands on a Manila Galleon and placed in the wall of Mission Dolores as a holy water font about the year 1791.

Collection of Mission Dolores

century. The standing candlestick in the sanctuary is of Ohlone manufacture. Among the most interesting 18th century Mexican paintings is an oil painting of "Our Lady and the Christ Child Arriving to the New World." Sometimes this painting has been humorously called "Our Lady Sailing through the Golden Gate."

Only recently through the research of one of our volunteers were we able to identify one of the figures in the painting as the Viceroy of Mexico, Bernardo de Gálvez. Behind the Great Reredos the wall is painted with decorations possibly created by Indian artists in 1791. These have not been visible to the public since the altar and its statues were installed in 1796. However, if you go into the attic, open a trap door, and hang upside down like a bat, you can still see traces of this Indian painting.

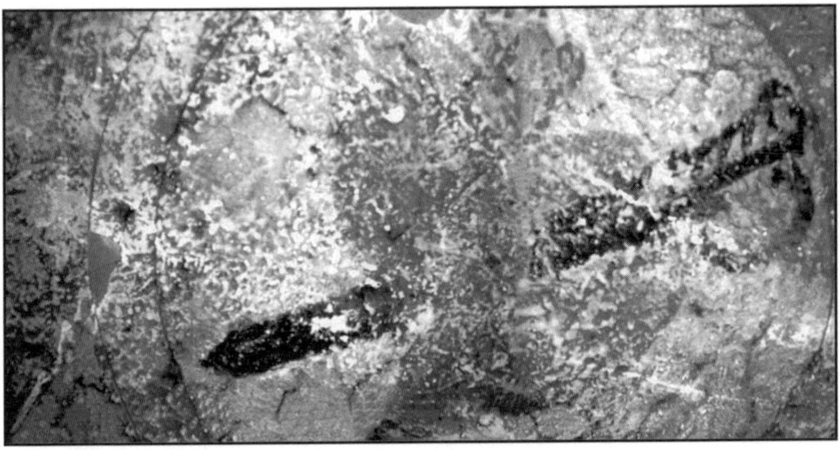

Ben Wood projected historic imagery of Mission Dolores onto the interior dome of the Basilica church. Ben Wood is a British born artist who creates site specific projects related to recreating historic images and superimposing video and still images onto architectural structures. His work celebrates history, layering images of past and present to create an alternative kind of electronic cinema. This project was a one of a kind exhibit, documenting and presenting historic images that relate to three centuries of life and culture at Mission Dolores. The projection also included images of the 1791 Indian wall decoration that has been hidden behind the Great Altar of Mission Dolores since 1796. These was the first ever digital color images to be displayed to the public.

Digital mural images by Ben Wood

Digital mural images
by Ben Wood

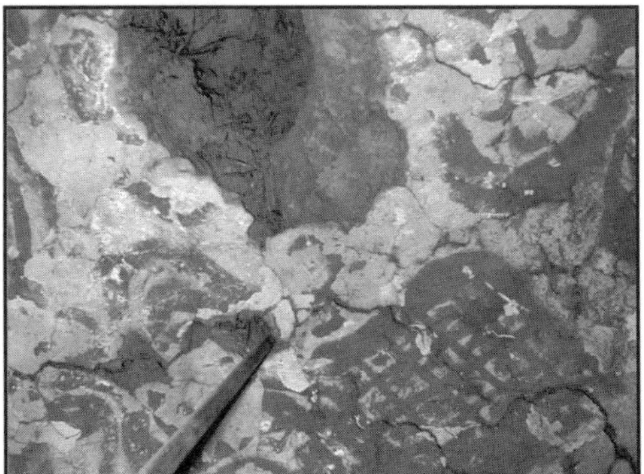

The Basilica

The parish church, commonly called the Basilica, was dedicated on Christmas Day 1918. It replaces the 1876 parish church destroyed by earthquake in 1906. Architects Frank T. Shea and John O. Lofquist designed the new parish church in the California Mission style and of concrete and steel to withstand earthquakes. Particularly noteworthy are the interior mosaics and stained glass windows depicting the 21 Franciscan missions of Alta California executed by the Meyer Company of Munich.

Umbrella and Bell. These symbolic items indicate that a church has been accorded the honor of "Basilica." Mission Dolores was only the fourth Roman Catholic church in the United States when it was named a Basilica in 1952.

Collection of Mission Dolores

Considerable care went into the design of the art and a letter from the Meyer Company to the pastor, Rev. Andrew B. Abrott, complained that each window had been redesigned once or twice and that the devalued American dollar made the project a "sour deficit." Some people visiting Mission Dolores for the first time think the Basilica is the old mission, because of its grand size and exuberant Spanish style. Some mistakenly call the style "Mission Revival." No mission in California was built on this scale or with such decoration and stained glass windows. It is California Mission via Hollywood.

There is more than a joke here; this is a story of the California of the imagination. In the early 20th century Californians wanted to attract settlers to California from other parts of the United States. Chambers of Commerce and real estate developers created an attractive myth of a Spanish paradise on the warm Pacific. This is the imagination at work. California was hardly Spanish, rarely a paradise and the ocean in Northern California is quite cold. This doesn't matter.

People were imagining themselves and creating a new image of themselves as Californians and were creating their history as they wished it to be. Incidentally, the population boomed and Hollywood became the mind's eye of America. The Basilica, in addition to being a place of prayer and pilgrimage, is a performance venue for such renowned groups as the Mission Dolores Choir, the Coro Hispano de San Francisco, Conjunto Neuvo Mundo, and Chanticleer.

Mission Dolores Cemetery and Garden

Mission Dolores contains one of the two remaining cemeteries within the city limits of San Francisco. All of the other cemeteries in San Francisco were closed in the early 20th century. Supposedly all of the bodies were respectfully exhumed and moved to the town of Colma, "The City of the Dead."

The magnificent Palace of the Legion of Honor overlooking the straights leading to the Golden Gate was built on a former cemetery. A contractor was paid to remove the bodies and rebury them. Just a few years ago while digging out a new basement at this museum hundreds of bodies in their coffins were discovered. Apparently the only thing the contractor removed was the headstones. Sadly, the statute of limitations had long passed as had the devious contractor.

The first burial at Mission Dolores was that of a nine-year-old daughter of the soldier Francisco Alvarez in 1777. The last burial was 1898. The original burial site was some three times larger than the now existing site and there has been some consolidation and removal of remains. Although there are only about 200 existing headstones, some 10,000 people were buried here, of whom some 5,000 were Indians.

Notable burials in the cemetery include early colonial families such as Noe, Sanchez, and Bernal. Luis Antonio Argüello, the first Mexican governor of Alta California, and Francisco de Haro, the first alcalde, are buried close to each other. The cemetery is also the final resting place of three victims of the Committee of Vigilance, James "Yankee" Sullivan, Charles Cora, and James Casey.

Inside the mission church are buried Lt. Moraga, Rev. Richard Carroll, William Leidesdorff, and three members of the Noe family. The Noes owned Rancho San Miguel, which extended over a considerable area of Noe and Eureka Valleys. The body of the founder of the Mission and Royal Presidio of San Francisco, Lieutenant José Joaquin Moraga, was laid to rest in the previous mission church after his death on July 13, 1785.

So deeply was he esteemed by the Franciscans that when the current church was dedicated in 1791, Moraga's body was reinterred beside the new mission church, close to the wall. As Padre Palóu recorded in the Burial Register, "The remains of the body of Don José Joaquin Moraga, founder and captain commander of the neighboring Presidio and of this establishment of our Father Saint Francis, were transferred from the old church to the new one, with all the pomp that was possible and becoming to his merits."

These and other handwritten documents and manuscripts are still preserved at Mission Dolores. Most of the remaining tombstones show that the people buried underneath came from Ireland. There are two reasons for all of the Irish in California of the 1850s: the great potato famine acted as a push from Ireland and the gold in the mines of California acted as a pull. (My own family came to America during this period.)

Sadly they chose the coal mines of Pennsylvania rather than the gold mines of California, but that is another tale. Irish are not the only people with tombstones. There are tombstones in French and a remarkable tombstone of a man with a Slavic name, but the inscription is in Italian. He was from Dalmatia which was then part of Italy.

Graves sometimes are decorated with weeping willows, angels or lambs. The graves of two firemen are decorated with firemen's hats, ladders and hoses. Obelisks were sometimes used. If the person died young it was carved to appear broken at the top because their lives had been "cut short." People often ask if the Mission is haunted.

> *"I tell children that the ghosts will get them if they walk on the grass or off the pathways. I tell the adults that the ghosts will haunt them if they pick the flowers or leave trash. I'm seldom believed, but they find it entertaining."*
>
> — Br. Guire Cleary

A cemetery memorial to a fireman who died in 1855.
Collection of Mission Dolores

Some people claim to have seen a woman dressed in late 19th century clothing walking around the cemetery and asking, *"Have you seen my husband?"* She is said to be the ghost of Ellen Aston who died in 1853. Believe that she would not be the first wife to wander about

The grave of Ellen Aston who died in 1853. She is said to haunt the cemetery.
Collection of Mission Dolores

San Francisco asking people if they had seen her husband, but they usually don't search after 150 years.

Mission Dolores Cemetery is also a garden. The roses surrounding the Arthur Putnam statue of "The Padre" are particularly beautiful in summer. Mission Dolores has been working to bring back part of our Indian heritage to the cemetery. Ohlone people built a traditional tule reed house in one corner and noted Ohlone basket weaver, scholar and artist Linda Yamane placed plants known and used by the First Peoples, such as soap root, willow, sedge and California poppies. With the plants she designed signage describing the plants and giving their Ohlone names.

The Native Sons of the Golden West placed a plaque on the wall of the mission paying tribute to the Ohlone Nation as the founders and builders of the mission and this community, thus making Mission Dolores one of the very few colonial sites in California explicitly memorializing the contributions of the First Peoples. Annual memorials and fiestas recall our history with pageantry and color.

The cemetery is also a beautiful garden with roses, and many plants that were used by the First Peoples. It is a place for rest and sometimes for reflection, but always a place of beauty and peace.

A group of school girls in traditional Chinese dress looking at the statue of "The Padre" by Arthur Putnam in the cemetery of Mission Dolores. C. 1940.

Collection of Mission Dolores

The cemetery garden at Mission Dolores. The statue of "The Padre" is by noted California sculpture, Arthur Putnam.

Collection of Mission Dolores

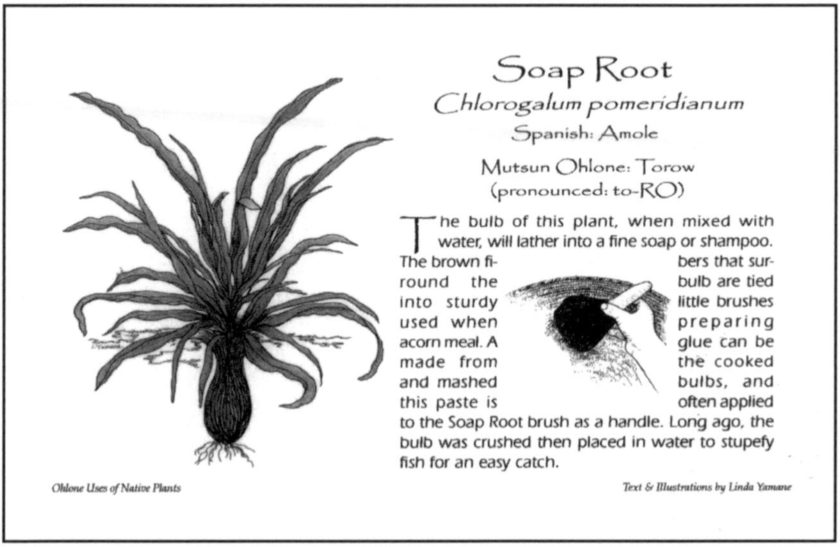
Soap Root
Chlorogalum pomeridianum
Spanish: Amole
Mutsun Ohlone: Torow
(pronounced: to-RO)
The bulb of this plant, when mixed with water, will lather into a fine soap or shampoo. The brown fibers that surround the bulb are tied into sturdy little brushes used when preparing acorn meal. A glue can be made from the cooked and mashed bulbs, and this paste is often applied to the Soap Root brush as a handle. Long ago, the bulb was crushed then placed in water to stupefy fish for an easy catch.
Ohlone Uses of Native Plants
Text & Illustrations by Linda Yamane

Signage for native plants in the Cemetery-Garden made by Ohlone scholar, basket weaver and artist, Linda Yamane in 2001. The description includes Indian use of the plant and its name in an Ohlone language.

Collection of Mission Dolores.

Modern Mission

The first democratic elections for alcaldes in Alta California occurred in 1779 when Indian neophytes were placed in office. This election was over the objections of Mission President Junípero Serra and at the insistence of Governor de Neves. Political controversy is one reliable aspect about life in San Francisco! In order to recall this event, and give honor and remembrance to the First Peoples, Mission Dolores reinstituted the custom of appointing Indian alcaldes.

These annual celebrations are full of drama. Indian customs, such as the placement of candles in abalone shells, incensing the participants with burning sweet grass, the performance of Indian chants and dances and the Indian Blessing of the Directions are often incorporated. Honorary alcaldes carry the traditional alcalde's staff of office. The staff of office used at Mission Dolores was a Bicentennial gift from the mayor of Vich in Catalonia, Spain.

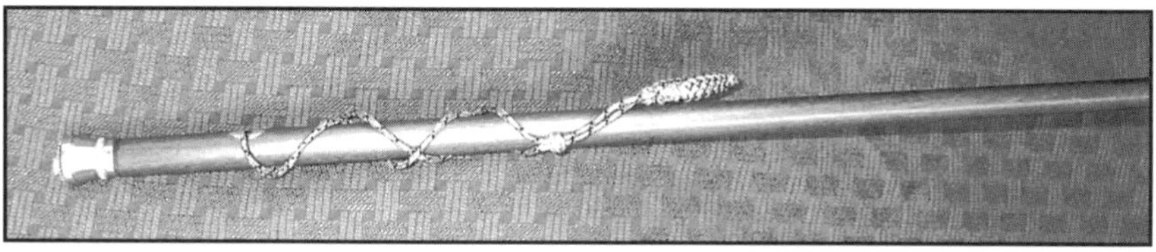

Alcalde's staff of office. This staff was given to Mission Dolores by the Alcalde of Vich in Catalonia, Spain as a Bicentennial gift in 1976. The first Archbishop of San Francisco, James S. Alemany, O.P. was a native of Vich.
Collection of Mission Dolores

Vich was the birthplace of San Francisco's first archbishop, James Sadoc Alemany, O.P. It is just such rituals that connect us with the stories of our Indian and Spanish Empire ancestors and the founders of the community we call San Francisco.

Historic Mission Dolores has been recognized as a landmark by both the City of San Francisco and the State of California. The Old Mission welcomes thousands of tourists, visitors, pilgrims and school children every year. Its beauty has captured the imagination of poets (Bret Hart, "The Bells of Mission Dolores"), film makers (Alfred Hitchcock, "Vertigo"), and rock musicians (Jerry Garcia, "Mission in the Rain".)

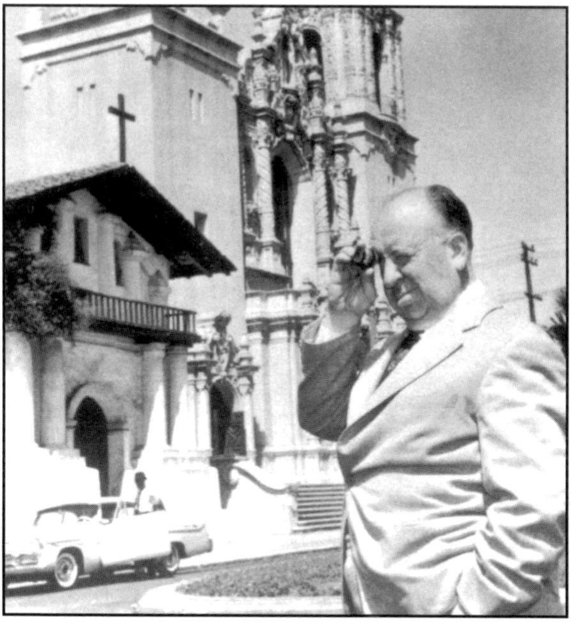

Alfred Hitchcock with a view of the Mission Dolores in the background.
Collection of Mission Dolores

The Lourdes Grotto at Mission Dolores Cemetery. Although no longer in existence, it ca still be seen in Alfred Hitchcock's film, "Vertigo."
Collection of Mission Dolores

It was not unusual for devout women to have their wedding gowns made into vestments for use by the priest during liturgical ceremonies or for decoration of the altar. Mission Dolores has a tabernacle veil in its collection that was once part of a wedding gown.

1933. A wedding inside the Old Mission.
Collection of Mission Dolores

Other Arts

Much of the art of the California Missions is directly related to the rituals of Roman Catholic worship and especially the liturgy of the Eucharist. Simple items of everyday usage in the Mediterranean world of the first century A.D., evolved into highly valuable, elaborately made and often beautiful liturgical objects. Sadly, three of Mission Dolores' most valuable treasures, a silver monstrance, missal stand and a chalice were stolen in 1987. These were said to have been gifts to Mission Dolores from Padre Junípero Serra. The reproductions are an echo of that lost treasure.

Replica of the Serra Monstrance stolen from Mission Dolores in 1987.

Collection of Mission Dolores.

The work of the goldsmith, silversmith and jeweler did not stop when the padres left. Every age has made its contribution as an offering of the imagination and hands to God. Sometimes the imagination is used to find a way around difficult situations. Many of the finest liturgical work in the world has been created by German artists. The stained glass windows and mosaics of the Basilica are an example of that art. There is a particularly fine monstrance (a gold or silver object used to display the consecrated bread) and chalice (a cup used to hold the consecrated wine) in the collection of Mission Dolores.

A story was discovered in the correspondence files about the chalice's manufacture. A pastor had some jewels he wanted incorporated into the monstrance and chalice. However, Germany was still occupied by the Allied Powers and bringing jewels through the military authorities was problematic. An obliging chaplain "smuggled" them through to the jeweler who then created a masterpiece. Notably, the Franciscans had been accused of smuggling goods around the Spanish Customs officers 150 years earlier to avoid the prohibition on trade with foreigners. It would be extreme to suggest that smuggling is a traditional art at Mission Dolores, but creative solutions to problems is the proof of imagination and the triumph over difficulties, especially bureaucratic ones.

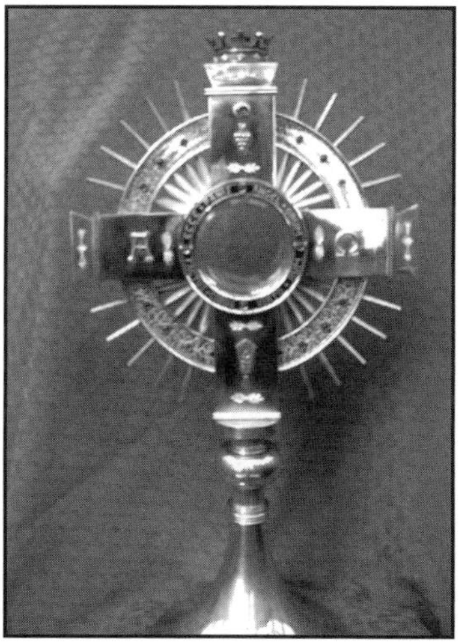

Mid-20th century German monstrance made with "smuggled jewels."

Collection of Mission

Among the most remarkable treasures at Mission Dolores are its liturgical textiles. Think of a bolt of Chinese silk traveling thousands of miles across the Pacific to Mexico and then up to California. Curiously, some of the more interesting old textiles at Mission Dolores were originally materials for well-to-do women's clothing. Some of the silk still glows with brilliant color after two centuries. Recently, attention has been given to preserving the textile work of early 20th century women who turned wedding dresses into vestments and altar hangings, created delicate works of lace and crochet and sometimes hand painted religious motifs onto altar and tabernacle hangings and banners. We know almost nothing about these women of Mission Dolores, but their loving contributions survive to this day and tell a powerful story in fragile threads.

Some items have remained in the collection to remind us as examples of bad taste. While some of the baroque style textiles show a dramatic, if not operatic flair and energy, one mid-20th century textile appears with sequins to be looking to Las Vegas for inspiration and would probably look better in the Liberace Museum.

The writing of history is an art. History is a work of the imagination, but hopefully not fiction. The first book of history written in California was written here at Mission Dolores by its founding pastor, Fray Francisco Palóu, in the 1780s. His book, News of California, was the first writing about the settlement of California by the Spanish Empire and the stories of some of its first Spanish Empire settlers and their relationships with the First Peoples. More than two centuries later this

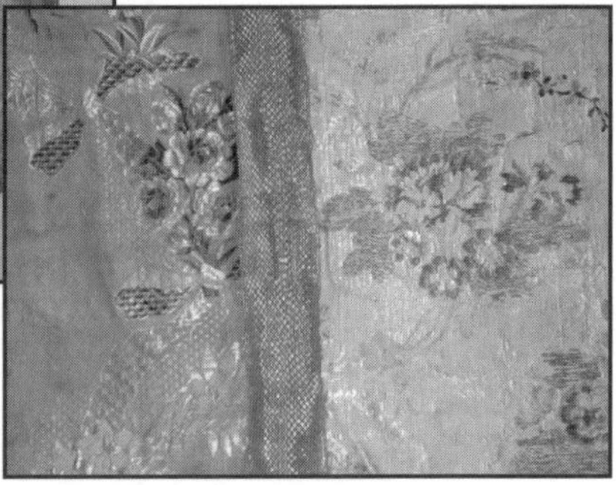

Circa 1750 pink silk brocade chasuble thought to have been pieced together from a woman's dress.
Collection of Mission Dolores.
Photo courtesy of De Young Textile Conservation Laboratory.

small history was written within a few feet of where Padre Palóu wrote his history.

The California Missions have captured the imagination ever since they first opened their doors. The late 19th century brought a new type of pilgrim to California: the tourist. Since America does not have majestic and ancient cathedrals as in Europe, our tourist destinations include adobe churches and the natural cathedrals of the towering Redwoods. The construction of the railroads made tourism convenient and

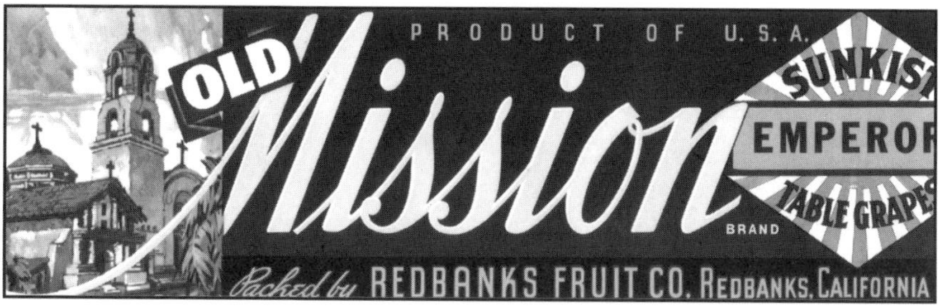

Fruit crate label for Old Mission brand table grapes with an image of the Basilica and Mission as they appeared circa 1920.
Collection of Mission Dolores.

relatively inexpensive.

It was not long before souvenirs of the California Missions appeared. Some were amusing and whimsical; others just cheap, but all allowed the tourist to take home a piece of California's treasured and romantic missions. Much of the pictorial documentation of the appearance of the mission has been saved in postcards. The California Missions also worked on the imaginations of Californians who incorporated the missions into popular culture as advertising California products.

There was Mission Dolores Spaghetti, Mission Coffee, and even a whiskey bottle in the shape of Mission Dolores. The romance and charm of the missions was sold to the rest of the United States by incorporating

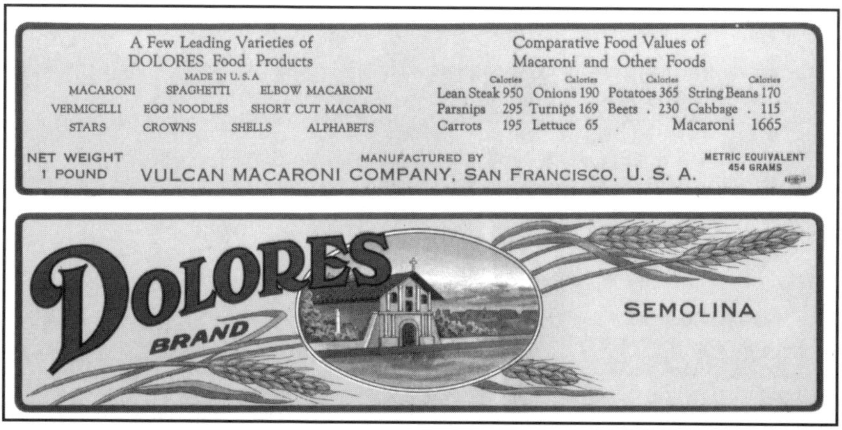

Mission Dolores brand spaghetti.
Collection of Mission Dolores.

Examples of Mission Dolores souvenirs: Chinese snuff bottle, juice glass, wooden model, and floating candle lights.
Collection of Mission Dolores

mission images on such items as grape boxes and dried fruit boxes. With modern transportation, fresh fruit is available all over the United States in all seasons at relatively low cost. However, before air transport a box of dried fruit coming to the East Coast from California in a wooden box decorated with California missions was highly exotic and the empty boxes would be used for storing personal items for years.

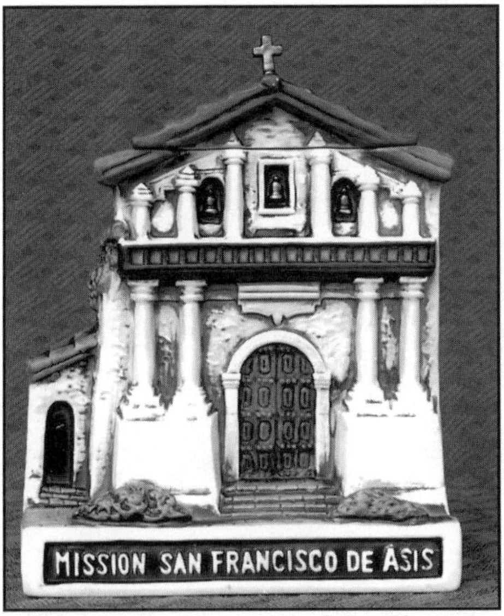

Mission Dolores as popular culture. A whiskey bottle in the shape of the old mission.
Collection of Mission Dolores

Every year tens of thousands of people take in the beauty of Mission Dolores. They admire her architecture and art, the peace inside its walls and cemetery, and the continuous history of living the Franciscan motto, ***"La Paz y Bien," Peace and All Good.***

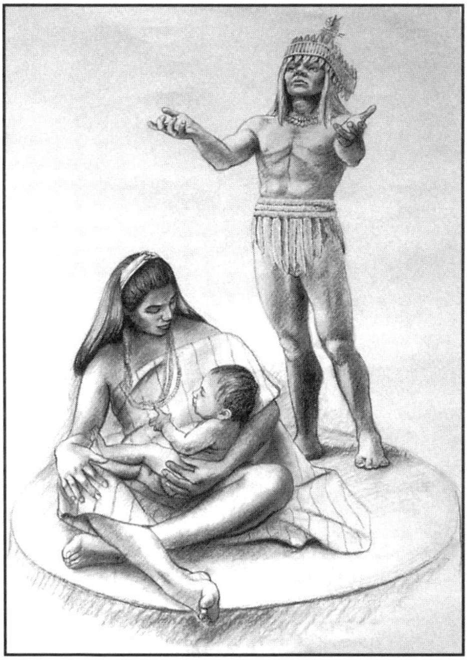

There is exactly one phrase from the language of the Ramaytush Ohlone who were the aboriginal inhabitants of San Francisco on any public marker in this city. It comes from a wooden plaque commemorating the first location of Mission Dolores. Would it be worth including? I usually include it with the beautiful sketch of the Ohlone family monument that was never built at Mission Dolores.

I shman colma carac yonahiacho isha hachche ahmush owahto harwec irshah.

Sun, earth, sky, village, friend, alive: we eat drink, sing and dance.

Ramaytush Ohlone language from the Ohlone marker in San Francisco.

Mission Dolores

APPENDICIES

POSTCARDS & POSTER, EVENTS, GLOSSARY, BIBLIOGRAPHY, WEBSITES AND INDEX

Postcards & Poster

Christmas card with red berries and California Poppies. c 1912.
Collection of Mission Dolores

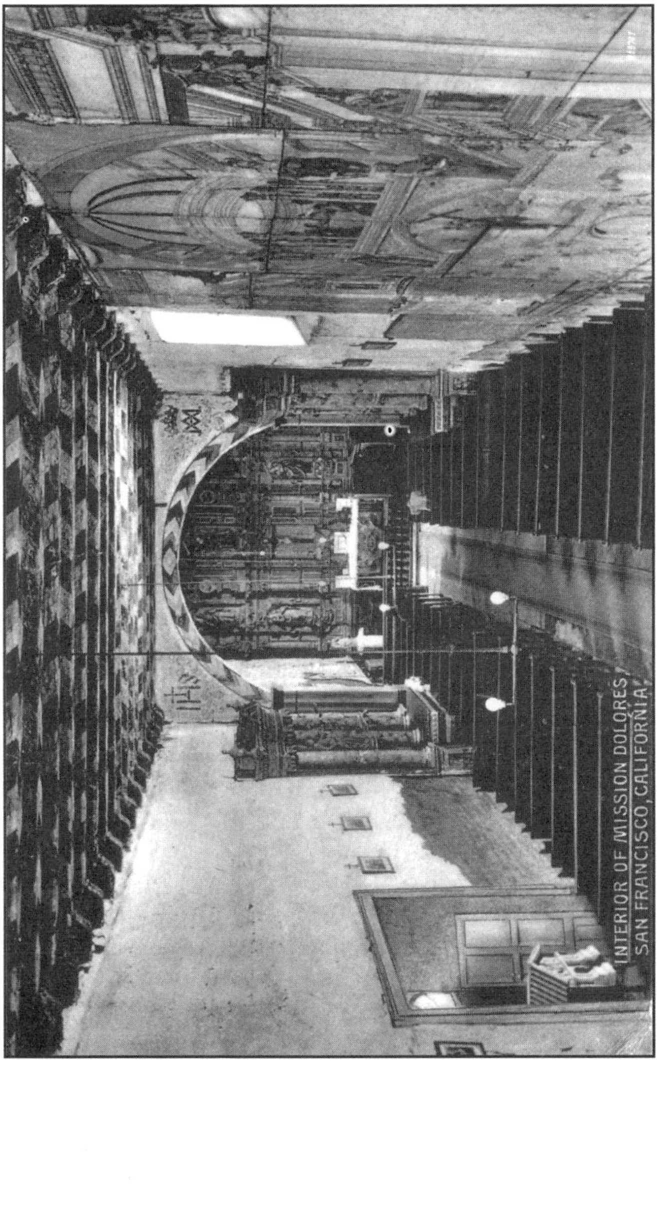

Interior of Mission Dolores - postcard. c. 1914
Collection of Mission Dolores

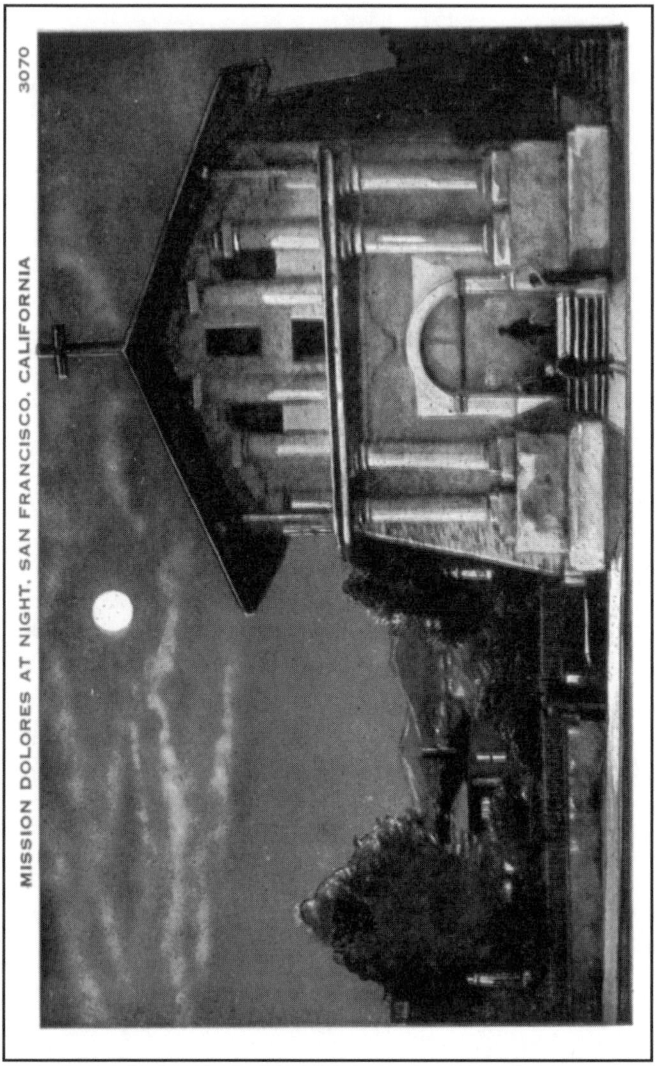

Mission Dolores at night under a full moon. - postcard. c. 1915.
Collection of Mission Dolores

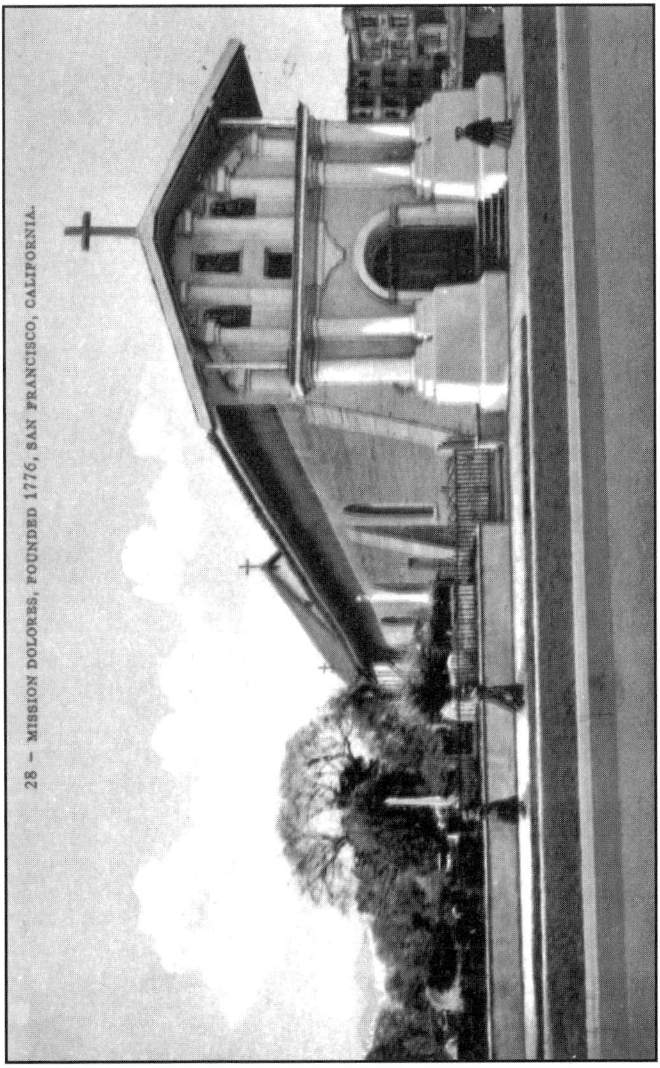

28 – MISSION DOLORES, FOUNDED 1776, SAN FRANCISCO, CALIFORNIA.

After the Great Earthquake and Fire. The parish church is destroyed, but the Old Mission and its cemetery remain - postcard.c. 1910
Collection of Mission Dolores

Mission Dolores just before the Great Earthquake and Fire - postcard. c. 1905.
Collection of Mission Dolores

Palm trees have been planted the length of Dolores Street. Palm trees are not native to this area, but look beautiful - postcard. c. 1919

Collection of Mission Dolores

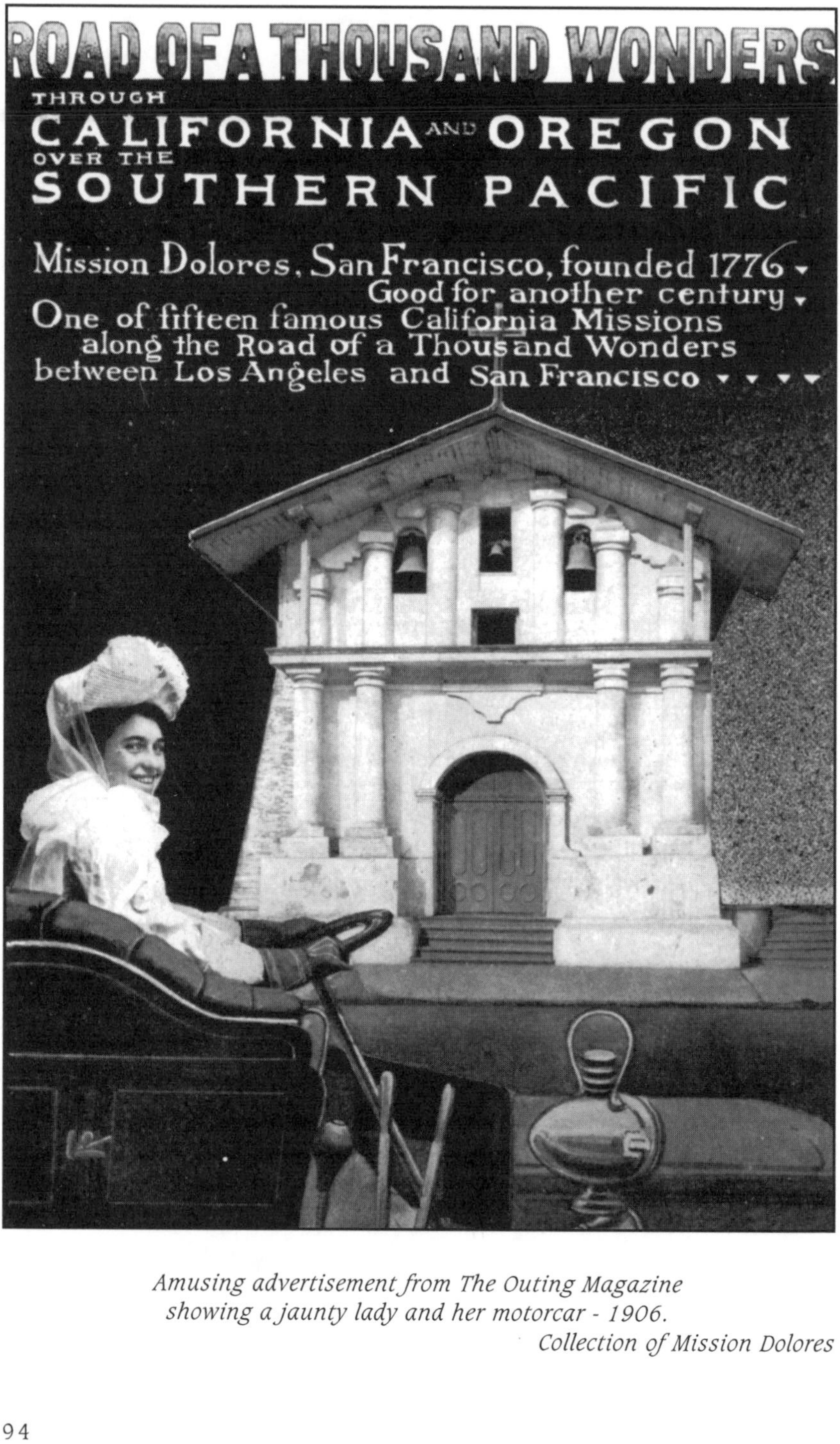

Amusing advertisement from The Outing Magazine showing a jaunty lady and her motorcar - 1906.

Collection of Mission Dolores

Events

Interestingly there is still a strong connection between Sergeant Ortega's family and Mission Dolores even today. One of his descendants is an Ohlone elder, Jakki Kehl. In 2001 they built a traditional tule reed house was erected by Indian and Spanish descendants to mark the 225th anniversary of the establishment of Mission San Francisco de Asís. Many Californians have this double heritage from both Indian and Spanish Empire ancestors.

June 2001. Building a traditional tule reed house in the garden of Mission Dolores. One of these people had ancestors on the de Anza Expedition. The other three are Ohlone descendants.

Collection of Mission Dolores

Mission Dolores is still a place of meeting and sharing for the First Peoples of California. On November 23, 2002, the Rumsen Carmel Tribe of Ohlone Indians held a first ever "Cross Over Ceremony" at Mission Dolores. The Rumsen Ohlone people prayed and worshiped God in the dance and chants traditional to their people inside the old Mission Church. Prayer was made to the directions to welcome their ancestors and to assist in their crossing over to the next life.

"Photos courtesy of Rev. Alexander J. Lewis.

Glossary

Adobe:	A method of building with mud.
Alcalde:	Mayor or magistrate (Spanish).
Alta California:	Upper California, now the State of California in the USA.
Asistencia:	"Assisting" mission attached to a larger mission.
Baroque:	Highly decorated and elaborate style of art and architecture.
Basilica:	Used to mean both a style of architecture and a church that has been honored by the Pope as important in the history of the Roman Catholic Faith (Latin).
Californio:	A resident of California during the Spanish and Mexican period (Spanish).
Encuentro:	"Encounter" The meeting of the Spanish Empire and the New World (Spanish).
Enramada:	Under a shelter made from the branches of trees.
Entrada:	"Entrance." The arrival and settlement of the Spanish world into the Native World (Spanish).
Fray:	Friar, often used as a title (Spanish).
Franciscan:	Member of a religious community founded by St. Francis of Assisi.
Friar:	A member of the Franciscan order of monks.
Friary:	The place or house where friars live.
Laguna:	Lake (Spanish).
Mission:	A place where people are brought to Christianity. Also used to mean the church building or the larger community surrounding the church.
monjério:	Unmarried women.
Neophyte:	An Indian Christian during the Mission Era (1769-1846).
Padre:	Term of address for a priest (Spanish).
Presidio:	Military base in the Spanish Empire (Spanish).

Pueblo:	Town or village (Spanish).
Reredos:	The framework or ornamental niches often containing statues of the saints. Sometimes also called a retablo (Spanish).
Viceroy:	The King's personal representative in the government of Spanish Empire colonies (Spanish).

Bibliography

Bancroft, Herbert H. *History of California*. Santa Barbara: Wallace Herberd, 1963.

Bean, Lowell Jon, editor. *The Ohlone: Past and Present*. Menlo Press: Ballena Press, 1994.

Beebe, Rose Marie and Senkewicz, Robert M., editors. *Lands of Promise and Despair: Chronicles of Early California.* Santa Clara: University of Santa Clara Press, 2001.

Bolton, Herbert Eugene. *Font's Complete Diary. A Chronicle of the Founding of San Francisco.* Berkeley: University of California Press, 1933.

Boulé, Mary Null. *Mission San Francisco de Asís*: Merryant Publishing, 1988. *Ohlone Tribe.* Vashon: Merryant Publishing, 1992.

Cook, Sherburn F. *The Conflict Between the California Indian and White Civilization.* Berkeley, California: University of California Press, 1976.

Cowan, Robert Ernest. *Mission Dolores*. San Francisco: Eureka Press, 1916.

Davis, John F. *The Founding of San Francisco, Presidio and Mission*. San Francisco: Pernau-Walsh Printing Co., 1927.

DeNevi, Don and Moholy, Noel Francis. *Junípero Serra: The Illustrated Story of the Franciscan Founder of California's Missions*. San Francisco: Harper & Row, 1985.

Duggan, Marie C. *Market & Church on the Frontier*. Doctoral dissertation, New School, New York, NY, 2000.

Dwinelle, John W. *The Colonial History City of San Francisco*.Reprint of the 1867 edition. Ross Valley Book Co., 1978.

Englebert, Omar (Translated from the French by Katherine Woods). *The Last of the Conquistadors: Junípero Serra*. New York: Harcourt, Brace & Co., 1956.

Englehardt, OFM, Zephyrin. *San Francisco or Mission Dolores.* Chicago: Franciscan Herald Press, 1924.

Font, Pedro. *Font's Complete Diary*, trans. and ed. Herbert Eugene Bolton, Berkeley: University of California Press, 1931.

Forbes, Alexander. *California: A History of Upper and Lower California.* Reprint of the 1839 edition. New York: Arno Press, 1973.

Geiger, OFM, Maynard. *Franciscan Missionaries in Hispanic California: 1769-1848.* San Marino: Huntington Library, 1969.

Graham, Mary (editor). *Historical Reminiscences of One Hundred Years Ago. The Mission San Francisco de Asís.* San Francisco: P. J. Thomas, 1876.

Guilfoyle, Merlin J. *Dolores or Mission San Francisco.* San Francisco: Dolores Press, 1965.

Gutiérrez, Ramón A. And Orsi, Richard J. editors, *Contested Eden: California Before the Gold Rush.* Berkeley: University of California Press, 1998.

Heizer, Robert F., editor. *The Destruction of the California Indians.* Lincoln: University of Nebraska Press, 1993.

Heizer, Robert F. And Almquist, Alan F. *The Other Californians: Prejudice and Discrimination under Spain, Mexico, and the United States to 1920.* Berkeley: University of California Press, 1971.

Heizer, Robert F. And Whipple, M.A.. complied and edited by. *The California Indians: A Source Book.*Berkeley: University of California Press, 1971.

Hittell, Theodore H. *History of California.* San Francisco, California: Pacific Press, 1885.

Hutchinson, C. Alan. *Frontier Settlement in Mexican California.* New Haven: Yale University Press, 1969.

Johnson, Paul C. (editor). *The California Missions: A Pictorial History.* Menlo Park: Lane Book Company,1964.

Krell, Dorothy, editor. *The California Missions: A Complete Pictorial History and Visitor's Guide*. Menlo Park: Lane Publishing Co., 1981.

Langellier, John Phillip and Rosen, Daniel B. *El Presidio de San Francisco: A History Under Spain and Mexico, 1776-1846*. Spokane: Arthur H. Clark Co., 1996.

Langsdorff, George von. *Voyages and Travels in Various Parts of the World during the Years 1803-1807*. London: Henry Colburn.

Margolian, Malcolm (Introduction and Commentary), Monterey in 1786. *Life in a California Mission: The Journals of Jean-Francois de la Perouse.* Berkeley: Heyday Books, 1989.

Margolian, Malcolm. *The Ohlone Way: Indian Life in the San Francisco-Monterey Bay Area.* Berkeley: Heyday Books, 1978 and 2003.

McCumsey, Robert. *California Missions: Measured Drawings. Historic American Buildings Survey.* San Luis Obispo: Learning Windows Publications, 1999.

Merrill, George A. *The Story of Lake Dolores and Mission San Francisco de Asís*. Redwood City: The Hedge Printing Co., 1942.

Millikin, Randall. *A Time of Little Choice*. Menlo Park: Ballena Press, 1995.

Neuerburg, Norman. *The Decoration of the California Missions*. Santa Barbara:Bellerophon Books, 1996.

O'Kane, Thomas. *Sermon on the Occasion of the 160th Anniversary of Mission Dolores*. San Francisco: Monitor Publishing Co., 1936.

Paddison, Joshua. *A World Transformed: First Hand Accounts of California Before the Gold Rush*. Berkeley: Heyday Books, 1999.

Palóu, Francisco. *Historical Memoir of New California,* vol. 4, trans. and ed. Herbert Eugene Bolton Berkeley: University of California, 1926.

Roberts, Helen M. Chamis and Lilote. *A Tale of Mission San Francisco de Asís.* Palo Alto: Stanford University Press, 1947.

Restall, Matthew. *Seven Myths of the Spanish Conquest.* New York: Oxford University Press, 2003.

Shoup, Laurence H. And Milliken, Randall T. *Inigio of Rancho Posolmi: The Life and Times of a Mission Indian.* Menlo Park: Ballena Press, 1999.

Thomas, P.J. *Our Centennial Memoir.* San Francisco, 1877.

Ward, Clarence R. *Mission San Francisco de Asís*, Washington: Historic American Buildings Survey, 1938.

Webb, Edith Buckland, *Indian Life at the Old Missions*. Lincoln: University of Nebraska Press, 1952 and 1982.

Webber, Francis J. *Mission Dolores: A Documentary History of San Francisco Mission*. Hong Kong:Libra Press. 1979. *The California Missions: Bibliography*. Hong Kong: Libra Press, 1986.

Williams, Jack S. The Library of Native Americans (series), New York: Rosen Publishing Co., 2003.

Williams, Jack S. and Davis, Thomas L. *People of the California Missions* ("Craftsmen and Craftswomen," "Indians," "Padres," "Sailors, Merchants and Muleteers," "Soldiers and their Families," "Townspeople and Ranchers."), New York: Rosen Publishing Group, 2003.

Magazine and Journal Articles

Palóu, Fray. "The Founding of the Presidio and Mission of Our Father St. Francis," trans. George E. Dane, *California Historical Society Quarterly*, XIX (June 1935).

Portman, Frank. "Pedro Benito Cambón, OFM: Mission Builder Par Excellence." *The Argonaut*, Volume 5 No. 2 (Fall 1994).

Rawles, James J. "The California Mission as Symbol and Myth." *California History*, Fall 1992.

Websites

California Historical Society:
http://www.californiahistoricalsociety.org
California Mission Studies Assn.:http://www.ca-missions.org
California Missions Foundation: http://www.missionsofcalifornia.org
Mystery of the Mission Museum:
http://mystery.sdsu.edu/main/index.htm
San Francisco Historical Society. & Museum:
http://www.sfhistory.org
San Francisco History Association:
http://www.sanfranciscohistory.org
Web de Anza: http://anza.uoregon.edu

Mission Dolores

Index

A

B

C

K

L

M

N

O

P

Q

R

S

Colophon

This book is set in *Caxton*, a Garalde typeface, designed by Leslie Usherwood for Letraset in 1981. *Caxton* is an old style face, having a large x-height, high-waisted capitals and short serifs. Designed to be used in journals, books and magazines, *Caxton* is easy to read in small point sizes.

The cover title is set in Tiffany, a Transitional typeface, designed by Ed Benguiat for the International Typeface Corporation in 1974. *Tiffany* is a blend of *Ronaldson* from 1884 and an early version of *Caxton* from 1904, having the exaggerated serifs of *Ronaldson* and the high x-height of *Caxton*. *Tiffany* is used for titles and display work.

William Caxton was an eary printer and the first to publish in English during 1471. He is known for publishing Chaucer's Canterbury Tales.

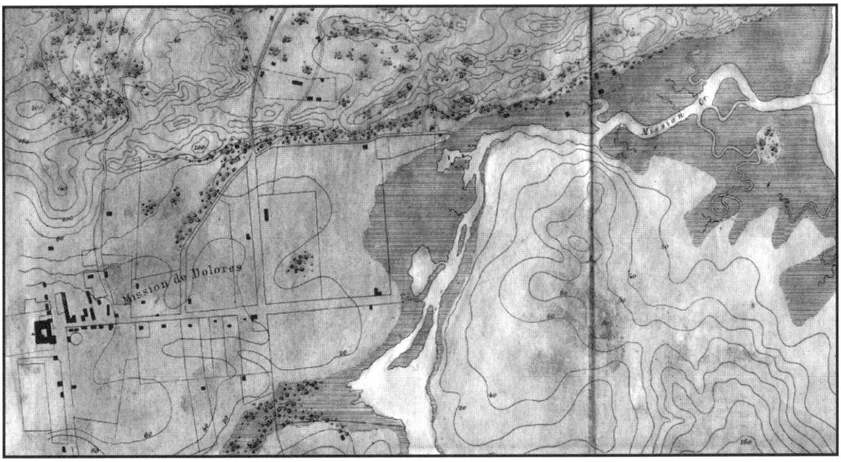

This illustration, taken from a recently discovered map of San Francisco, shows the Mission complex in 1853

California Missions Foundation

Help save California's historic missions:
Contribute to the California Missions Foundation
– a non-profit organization –

Name: ______________________________

Address: ______________________________

City/St/Zip: ______________________________

Phone: ______________________________

I wish my gift to be: ❑ shared equally with all the missions
❑ designated to preservation and conservation efforts at:

____
(Name your designated mission)

Amount: $______________

❑ Check enclosed (to California Missions Foundation)

– or –

❑ Credit card: ❑ VISA ❑ MC
❑ AMEX ❑ Diners Club

□□□□-□□□□-□□□□-□□□□

Expiration Date: □□/□□

Note: Address above should be the Credit card billing address

Thank you for caring!
Your tax-deductible gift is deeply appreciated.

California Missions Foundation
1007 7th Street, Suite 319, Sacramento, CA 95814
Tel: 916-498-0110, Fax: 916-498-0120
Toll Free: 877-632-3623, Website: WWW.SAVE-TH-MISSIONS.ORG